FOR ORGANS, PIANOS & ELECTRONIC KEYBOARDS

E-Z PLAY TODAY

44

BEST OF WILLIE NELSON

T0210262

Cover photo: ALAN MAYOR

ISBN 978-0-7935-0534-0

EXCLUSIVELY DISTRIBUTED BY

HAL•LEONARD®
CORPORATION

7777 W. BLUEMOUND RD. P.O BOX 13819 MILWAUKEE, WI 53213

BEST OF
WILLIE NELSON

Always On My Mind

Registration 10
Rhythm: Country or Shuffle

Words and Music by Wayne Thompson,
Mark James and Johnny Christopher

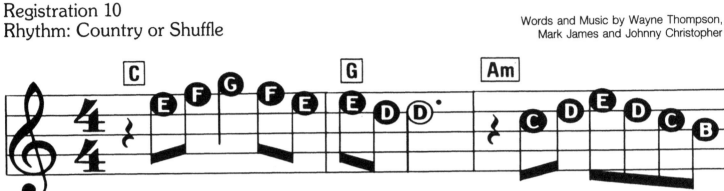

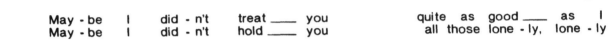

May - be I did - n't treat ____ you   quite as good ____ as I
May - be I did - n't hold ____ you   all those lone - ly, lone - ly

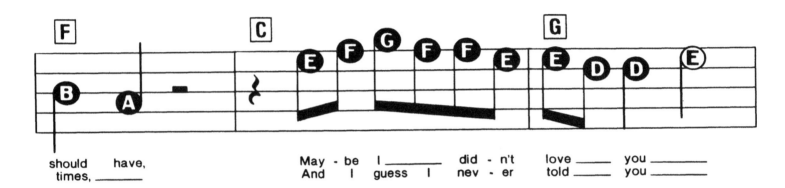

should have,   May - be I _____ did - n't love ____ you _____
times, _____   And I guess I nev - er told ____ you _____

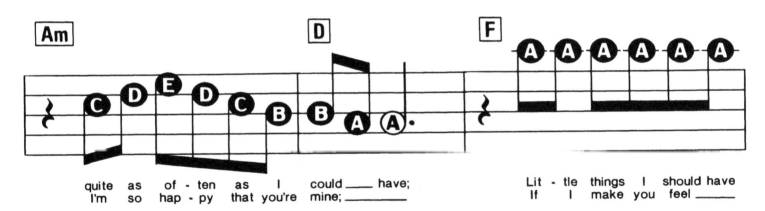

quite as of - ten as I could ____ have;   Lit - tle things I should have
I'm so hap - py that you're mine; ____   If I make you feel ____

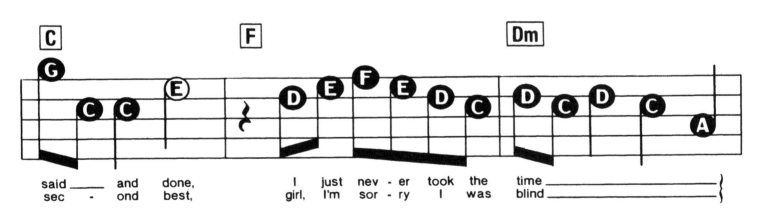

said ____ and done,   I just nev - er took the time _____
sec - ond best,   girl, I'm sor - ry I was blind _____

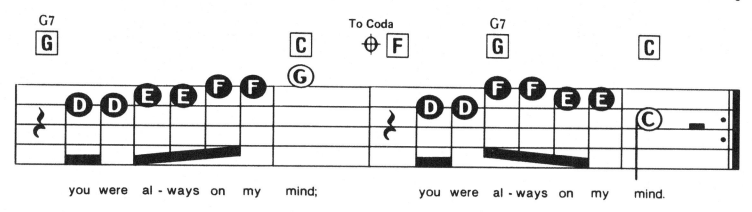

you were al-ways on my mind; you were al-ways on my mind.

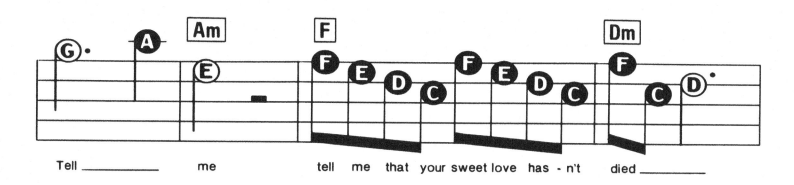

Tell _____ me tell me that your sweet love has-n't died _____

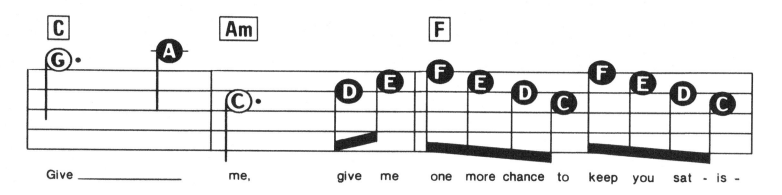

Give _____ me, give me one more chance to keep you sat-is-

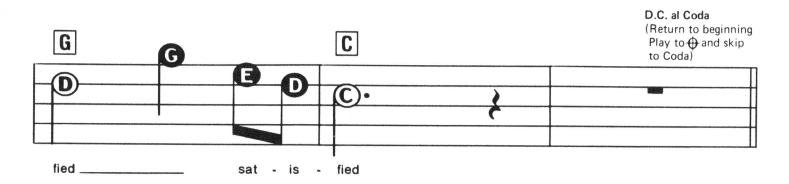

fied _____ sat-is-fied

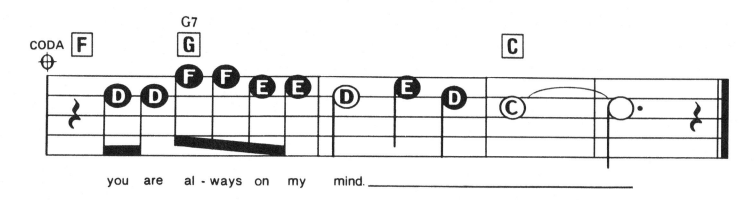

you are al-ways on my mind. _____

Blue Eyes Crying In The Rain

Registration 9
Rhythm: Swing or Country

Words and Music by
Fred Rose

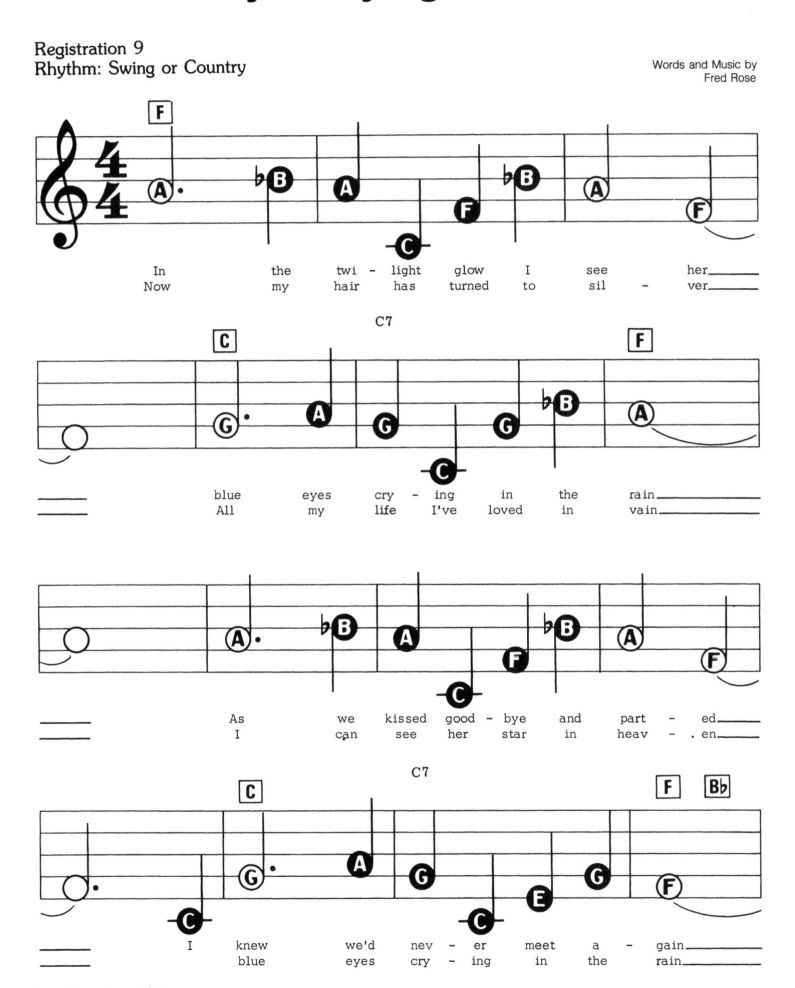

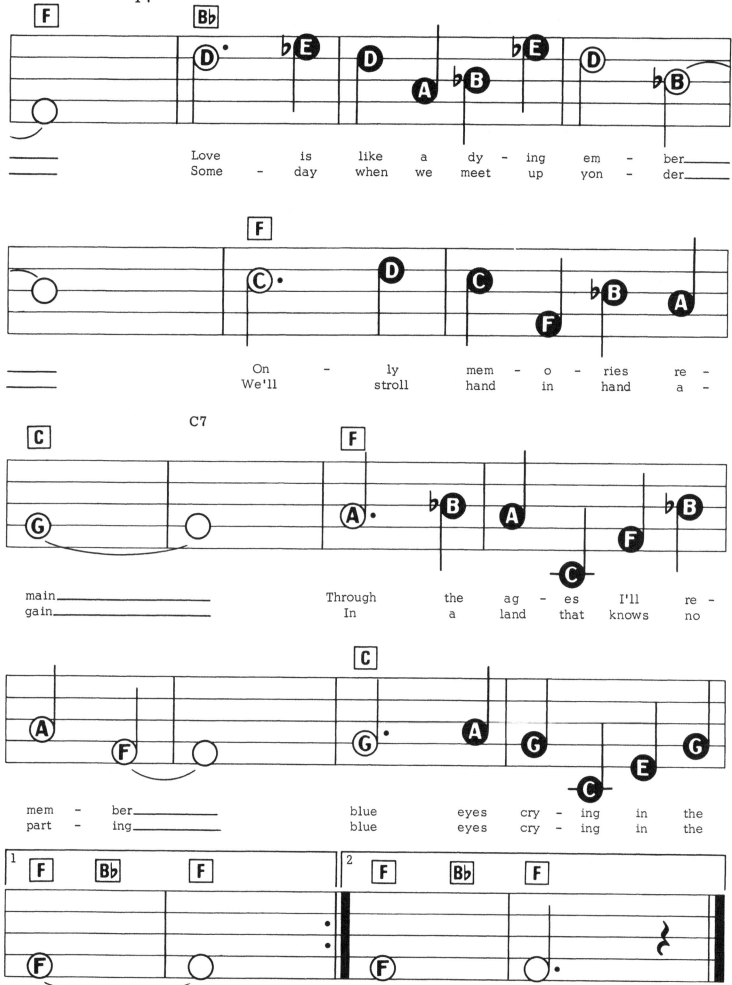

Love   is   like   a   dy - ing   em - ber
Some - day   when   we   meet   up   yon - der

On - ly   mem - o - ries   re -
We'll   stroll   hand   in   hand   a -

main_____   Through   the   ag - es   I'll   re -
gain_____   In   a   land   that   knows   no

mem - ber_____   blue   eyes   cry - ing   in   the
part - ing_____   blue   eyes   cry - ing   in   the

rain._____
rain._____

Comin' Back To Texas

Registration 4
Rhythm: Country or Rock

Arrangement by Kenneth Threadgill,
Chuck Joyce and Julie Paul

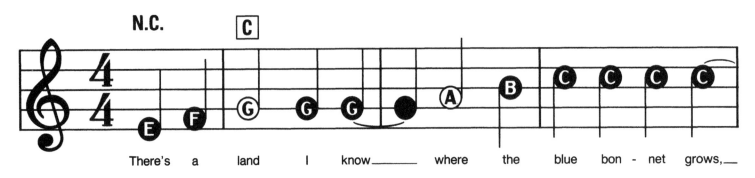

There's a land I know _____ where the blue bon - net grows,

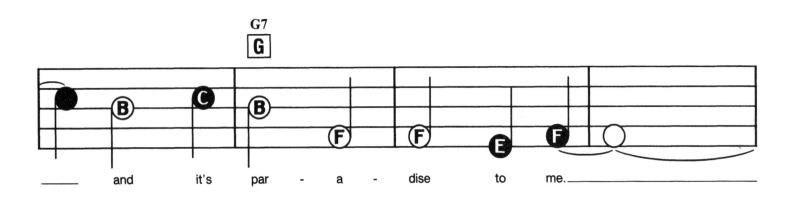

_____ and it's par - a - dise to me. _____

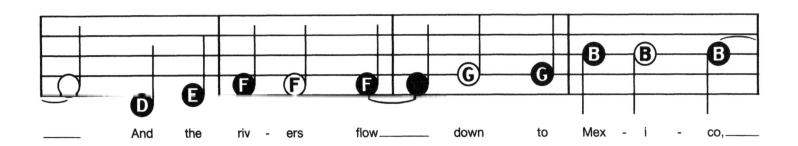

_____ And the riv - ers flow _____ down to Mex - i - co, _____

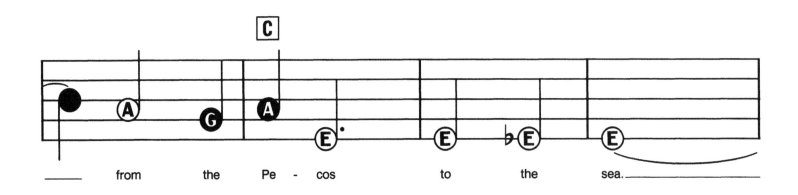

_____ from the Pe - cos to the sea. _____

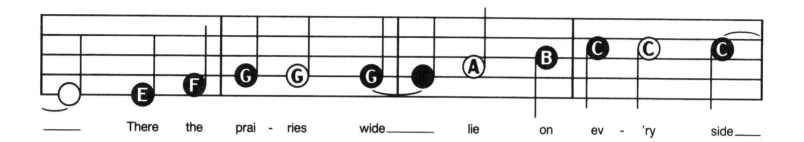

There the prai - ries wide_____ lie on ev - 'ry side_____

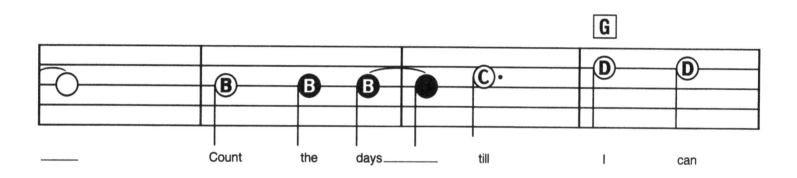

_____ and the moun - tain heav - en high._____

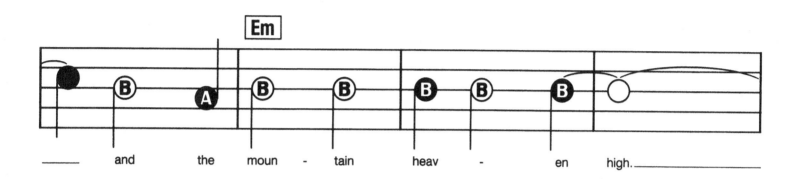

_____ Count the days_____ till I can

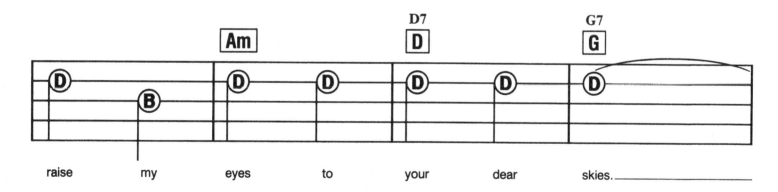

raise my eyes to your dear skies._____

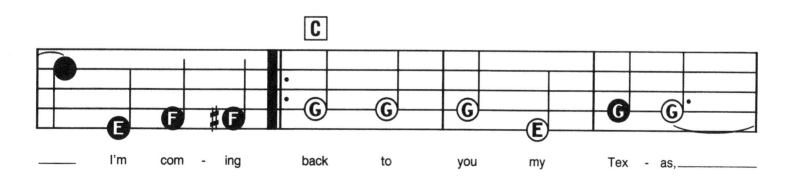

_____ I'm com - ing back to you my Tex - as,_____

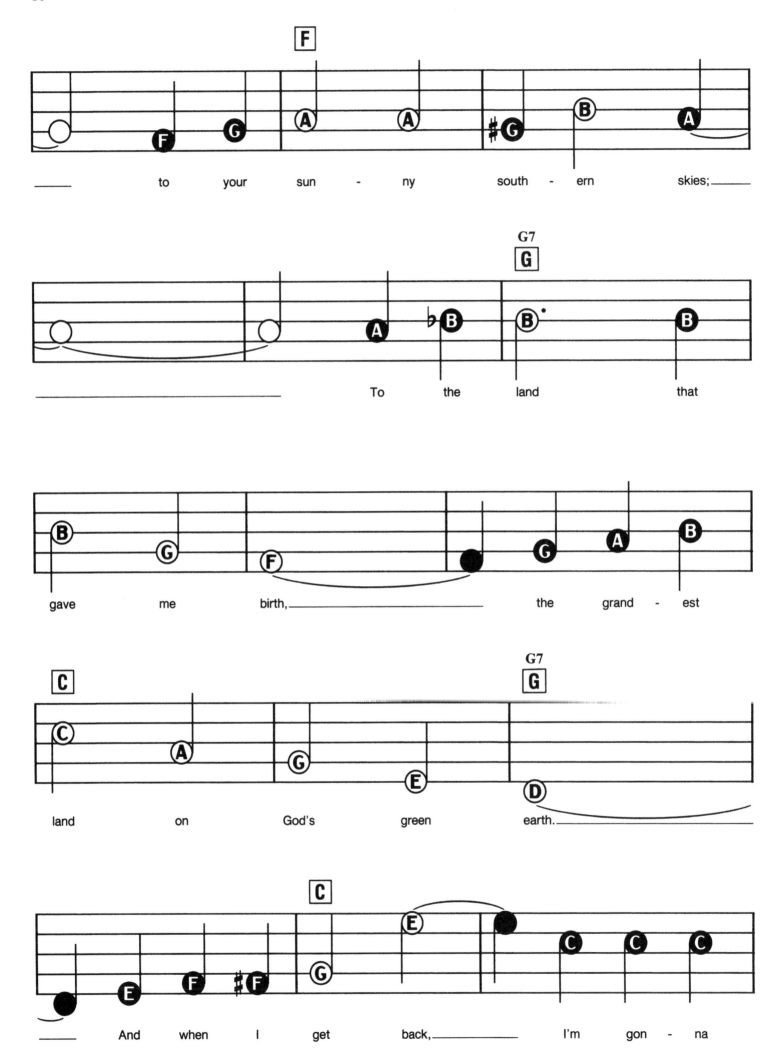

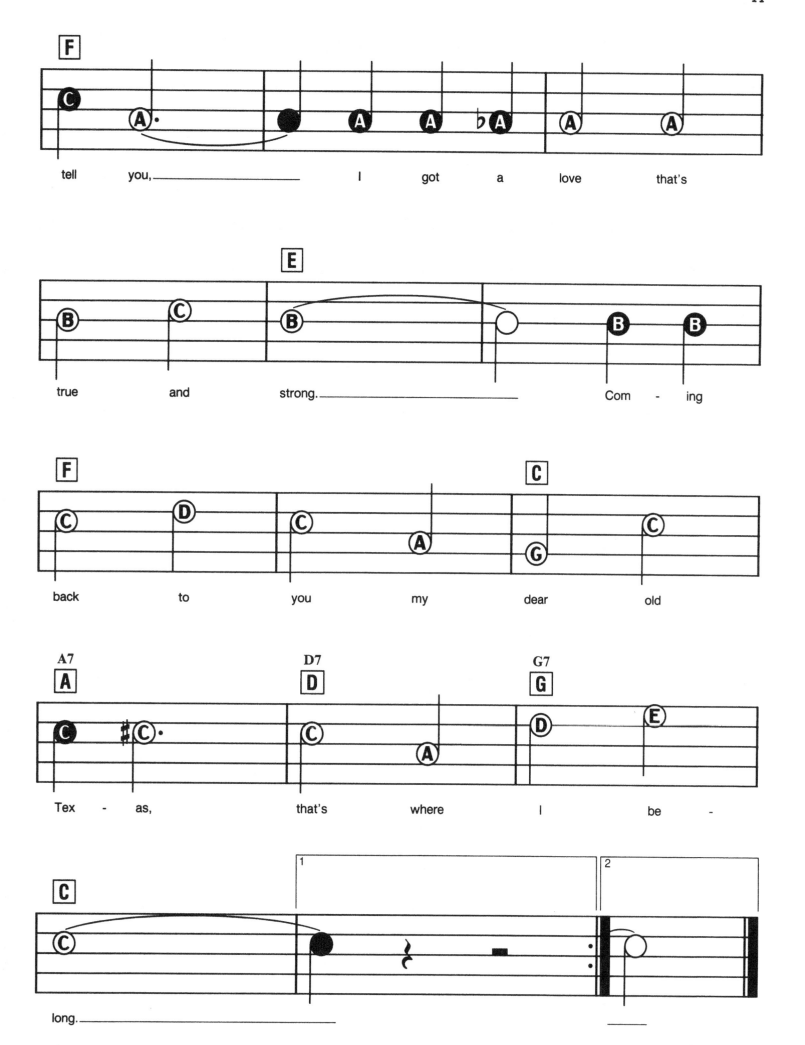

Crazy

Registration 2
Rhythm: Swing or Country

Words and Music by
Willie Nelson

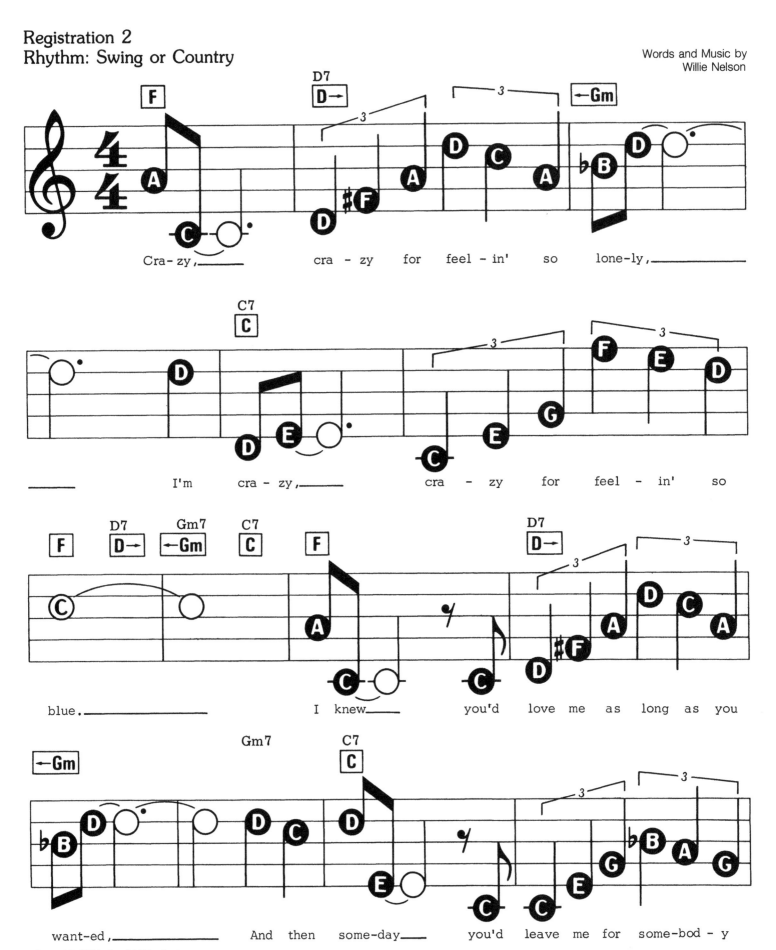

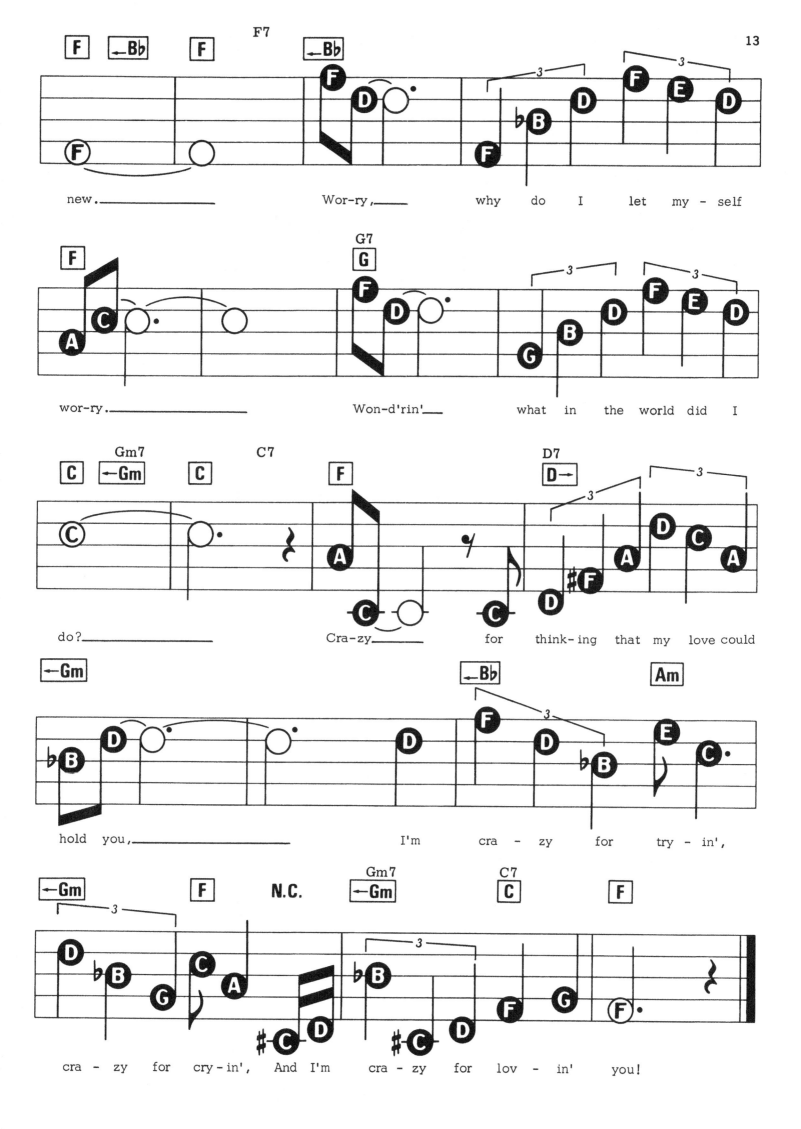

Faded Love

Registration 1
Rhythm: Country

Words and Music by
John Wills and Bob Wills

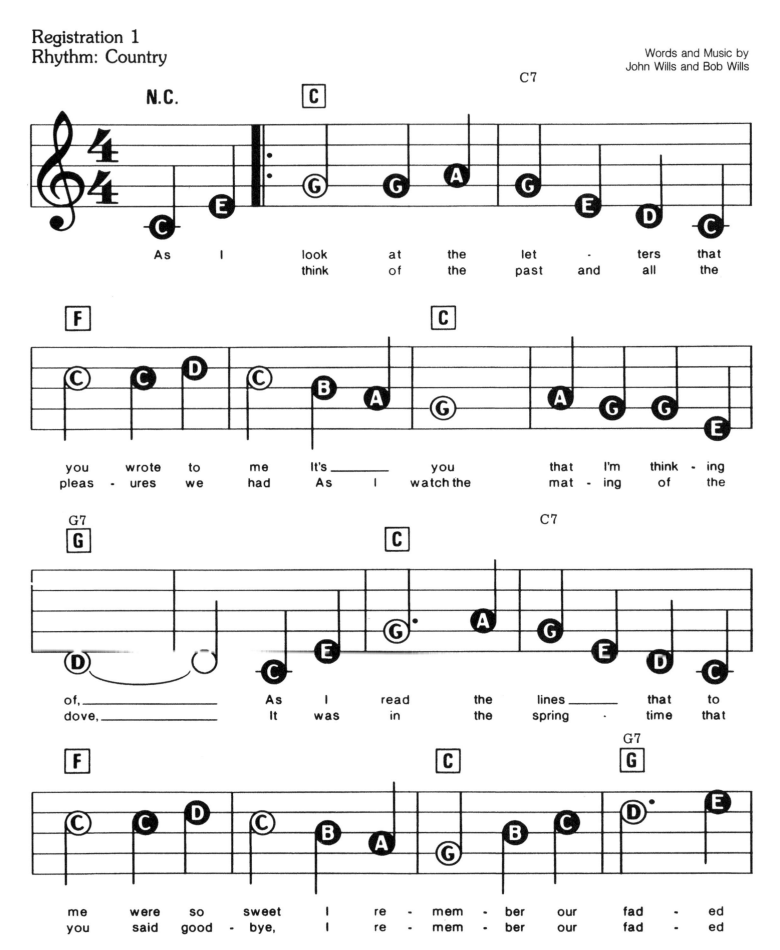

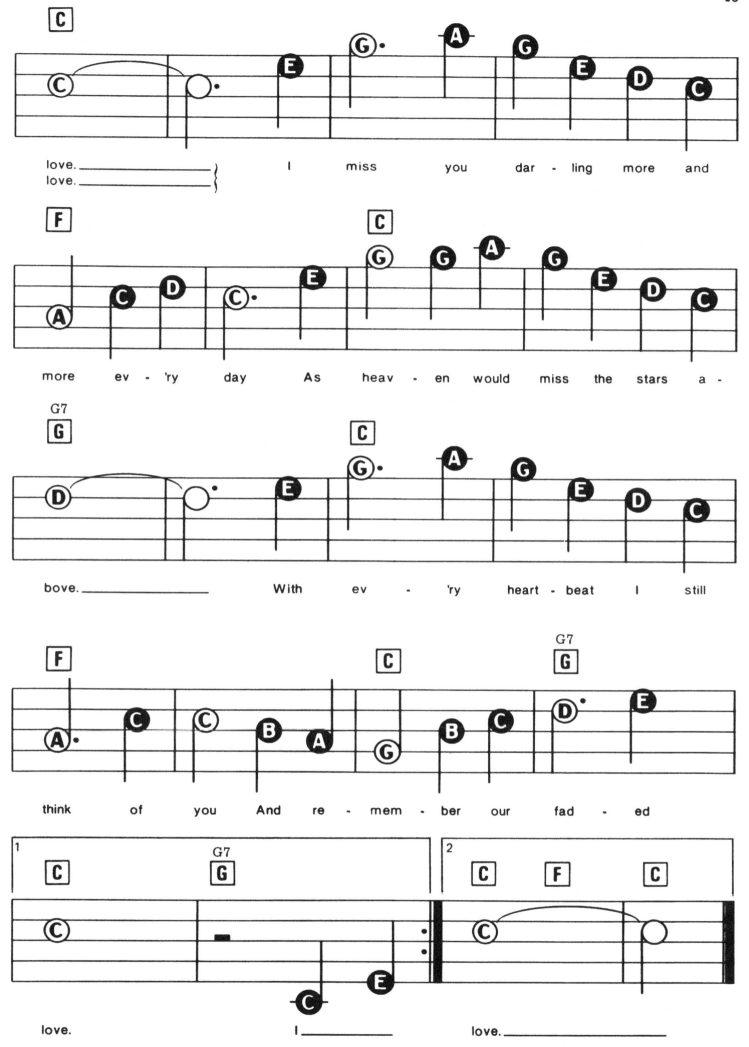

Funny How Time Slips Away

Registration 1
Rhythm: Country

Words and Music by
Willie Nelson

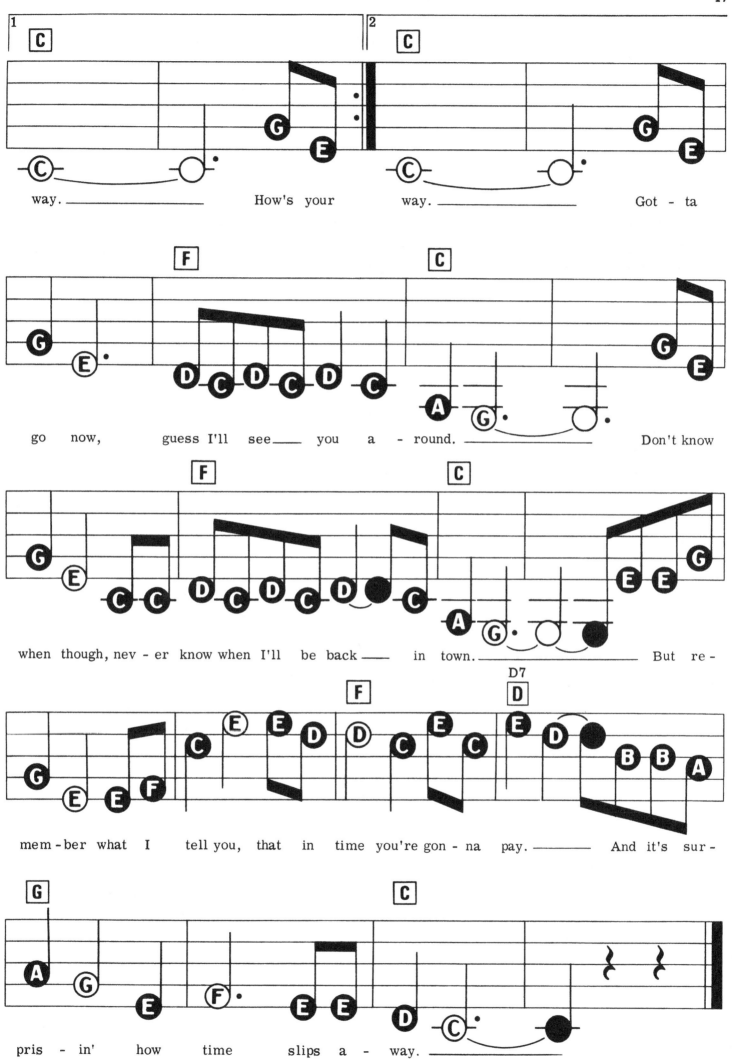

Georgia On My Mind

Registration 4
Rhythm: Swing

Lyrics by Stuart Gorrell
Music by Hoagy Carmichael

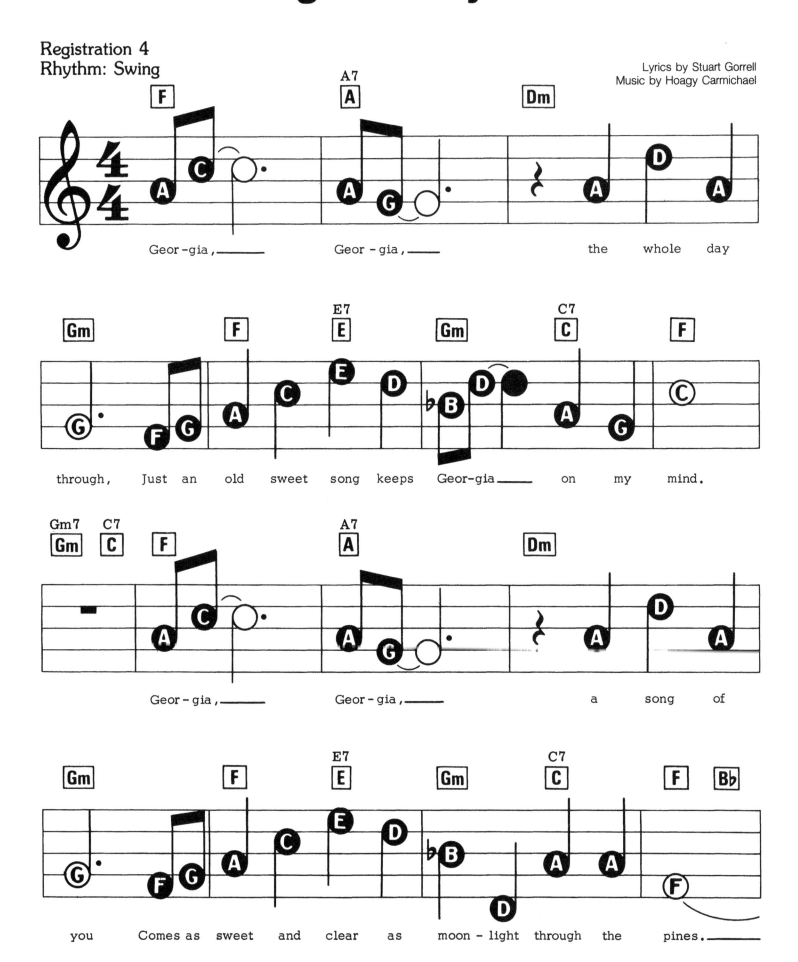

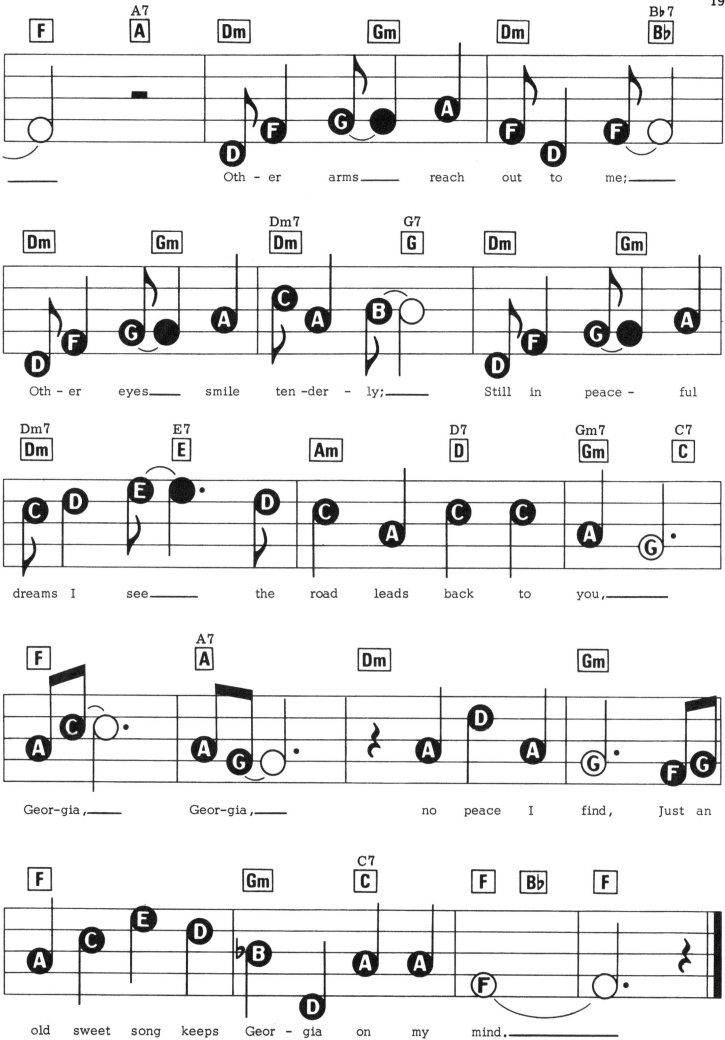

Good Hearted Woman

Registration 4
Rhythm: Country

Words and Music by
Waylon Jennings and Willie Nelson

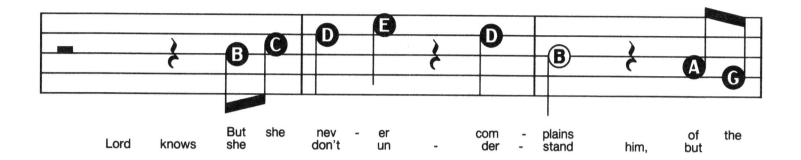

Lord knows But she nev - er com - plains of the

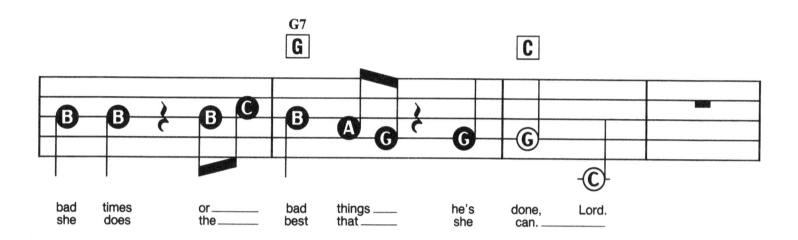

bad times or_____ bad things_____ he's done, Lord.
she does the_____ best that_____ she can._____

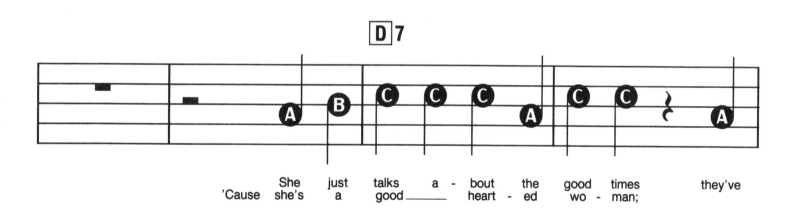

'Cause She just talks a - bout the good times they've
She's just a good_____ heart - ed wo - man;

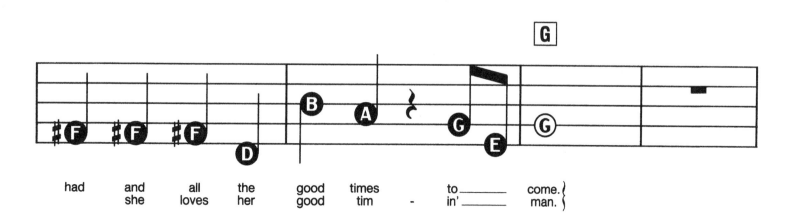

had and all the good times to_____ come.
she loves her good tim - in'_____ man.

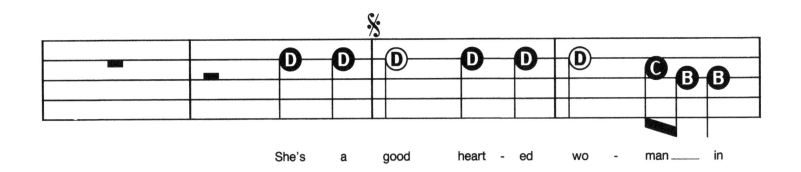

She's a good heart - ed wo - man ____ in

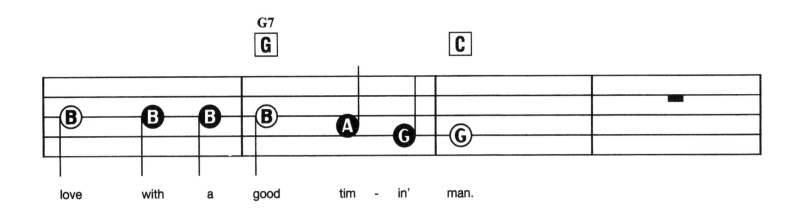

love with a good tim - in' man.

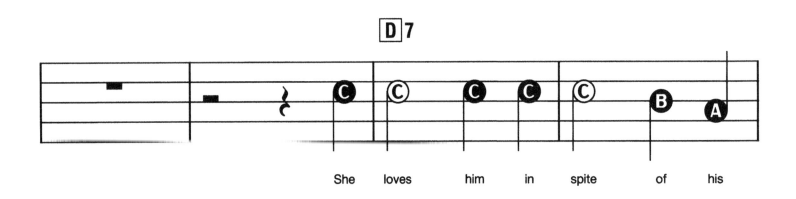

She loves him in spite of his

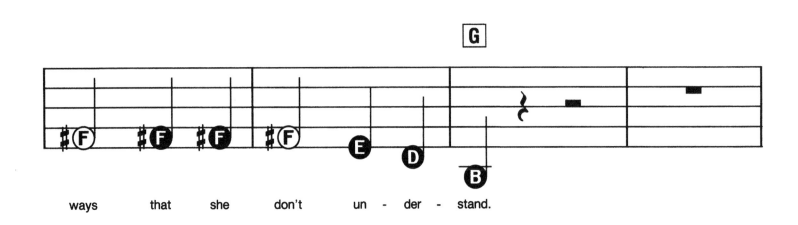

ways that she don't un - der - stand.

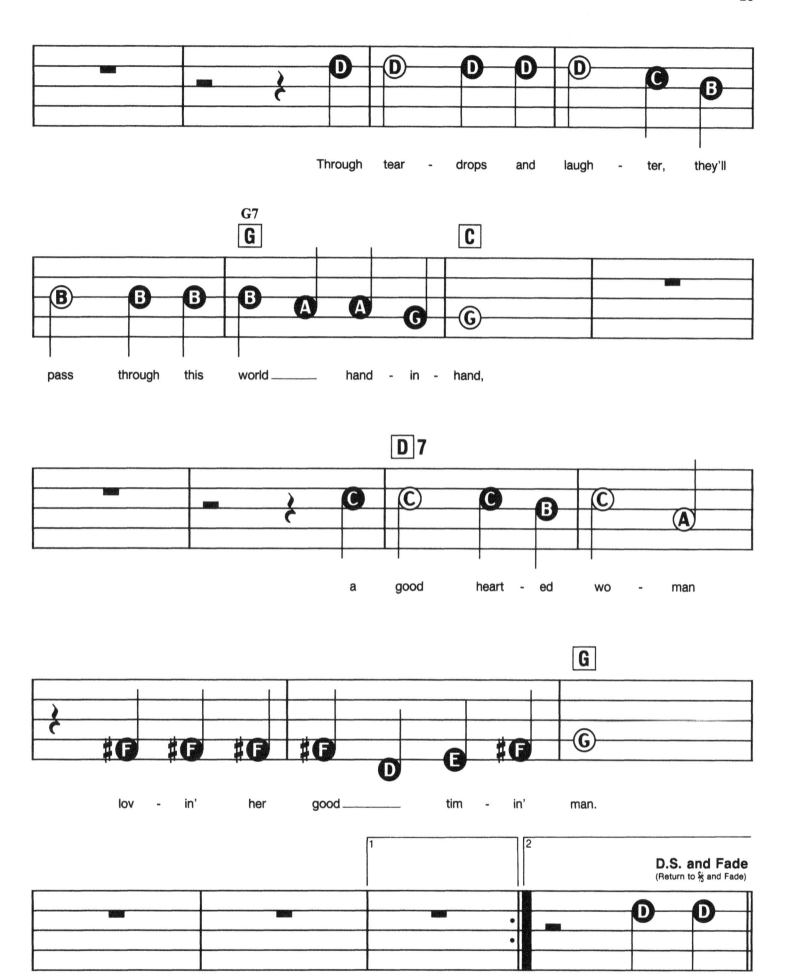

Good Time Charlie's Got The Blues

Registration 1
Rhythm: Rock or Country

Words and Music by
Danny O'Keefe

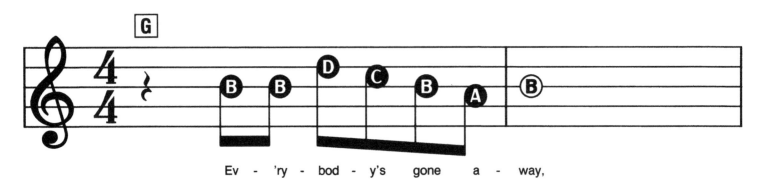

Ev - 'ry - bod - y's gone a - way,

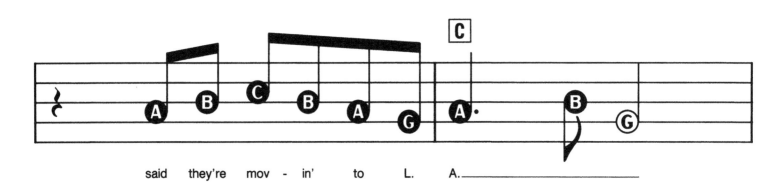

said they're mov - in' to L. A.

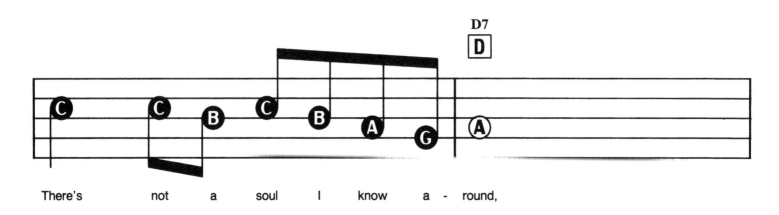

There's not a soul I know a - round,

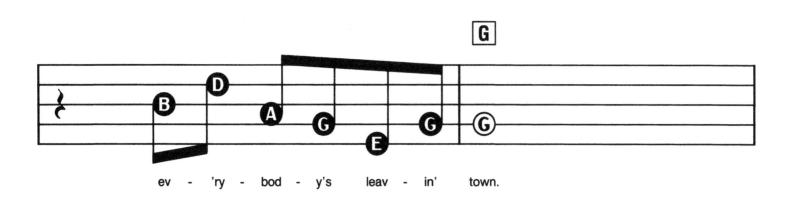

ev - 'ry - bod - y's leav - in' town.

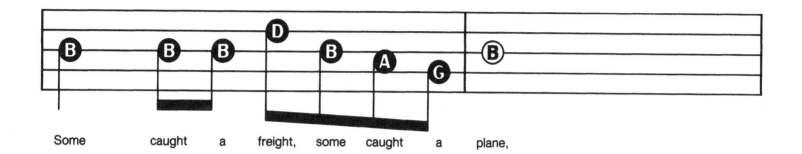

Some   caught a freight, some caught a plane,

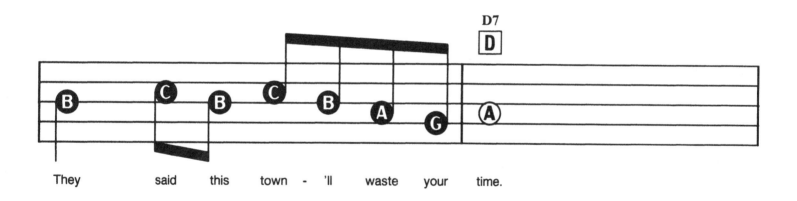

Find   the   sun - shine leave the rain._____

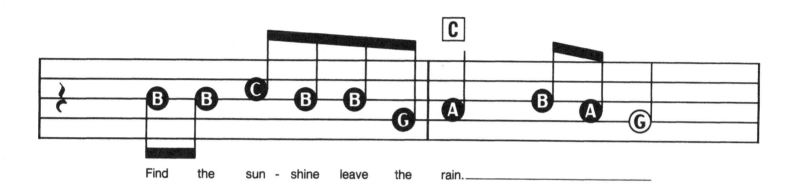

They   said this town - 'll waste your time.

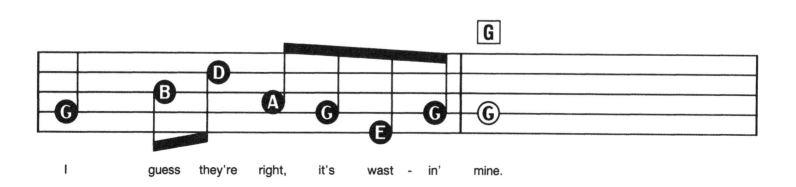

I   guess they're right, it's wast - in' mine.

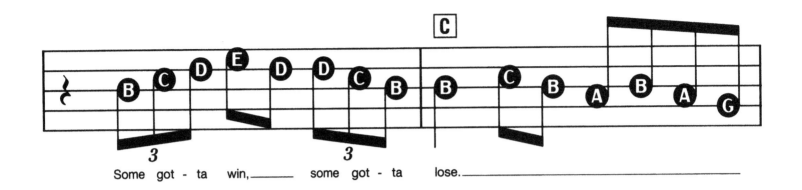

Some got - ta win,_____ some got - ta lose._____

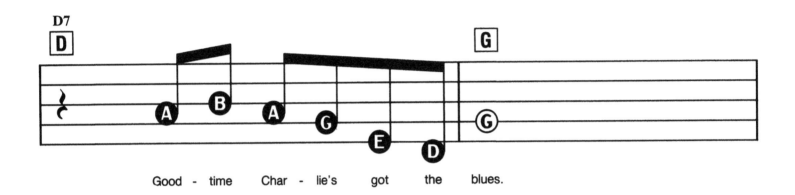

Good - time Char - lie's got the blues.

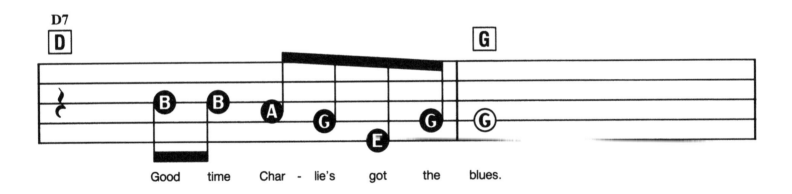

Good time Char - lie's got the blues.

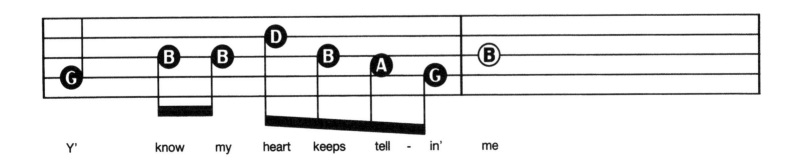

Y' know my heart keeps tell - in' me

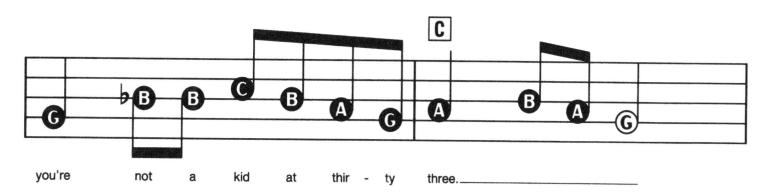

you're not a kid at thir - ty three.____

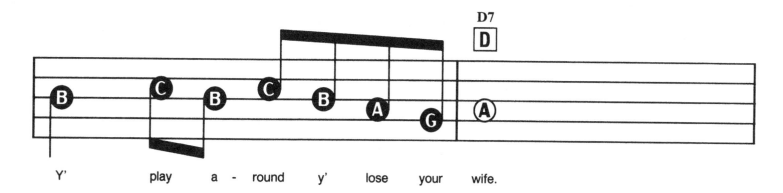

Y' play a - round y' lose your wife.

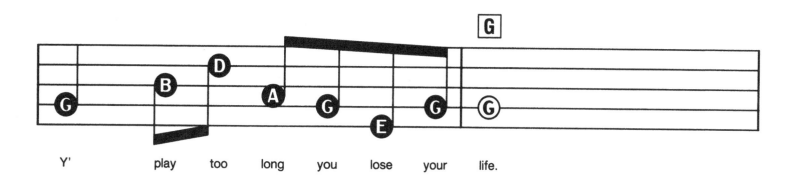

Y' play too long you lose your life.

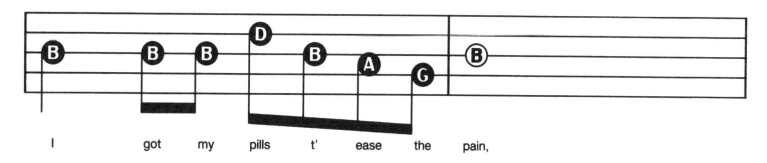

I got my pills t' ease the pain,

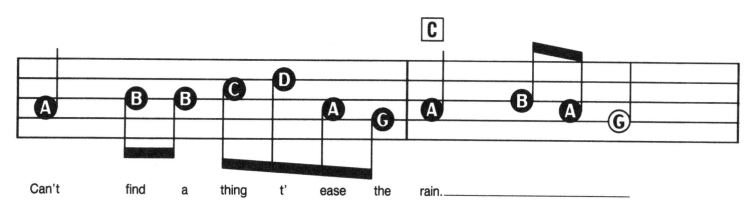

Can't find a thing t' ease the rain.____

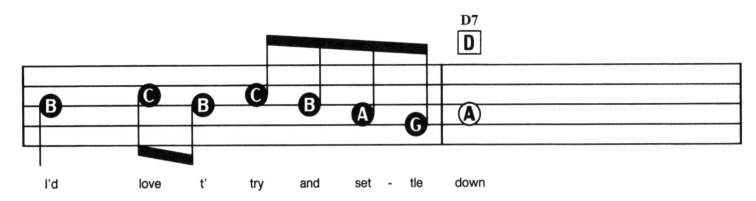

I'd   love t' try and set - tle down

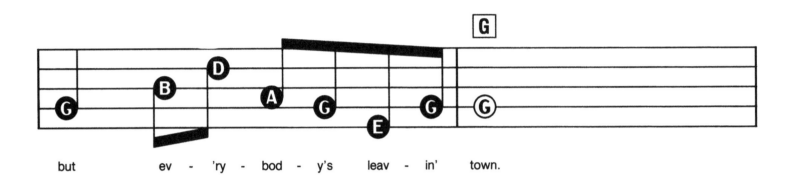

but   ev - 'ry - bod - y's   leav - in' town.

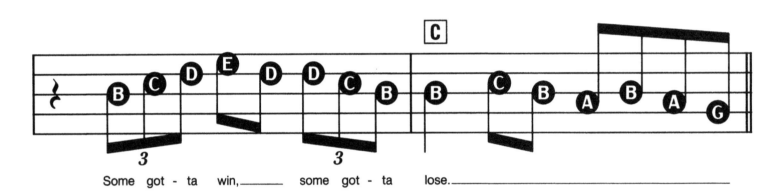

Some got - ta win,_____ some got - ta lose._____

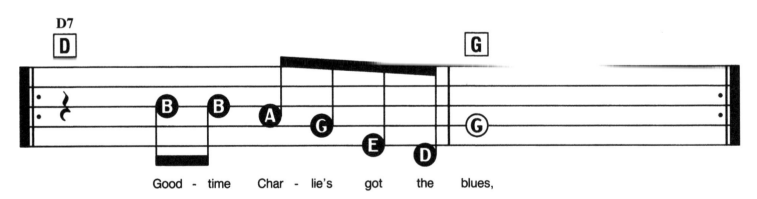

Good - time Char - lie's   got   the   blues,

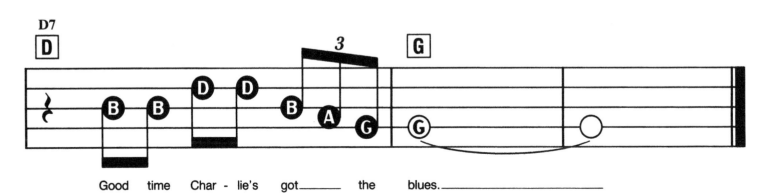

Good time Char - lie's got_____ the   blues._____

How Do You Feel About Foolin' Around

Registration 4
Rhythm: Rock or 8 Beat

Words and Music by Kris Kristofferson,
Mike Utely and Stephen Bruton

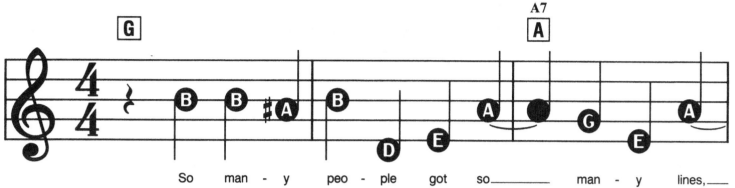

So man - y peo - ple got so_____ man - y lines,_____

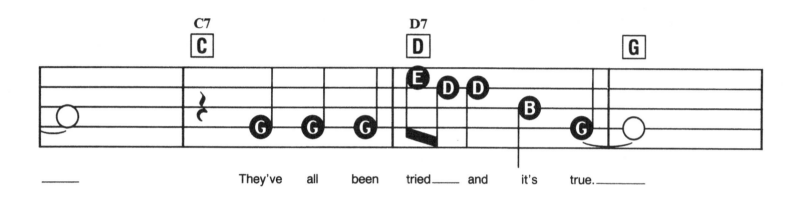

_____ They've all been tried_____ and it's true._____

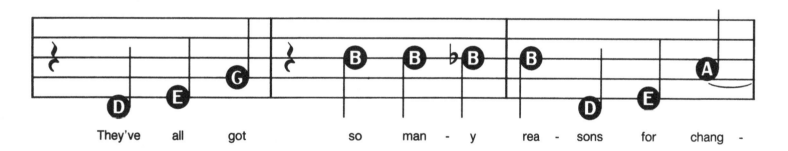

They've all got so man - y rea - sons for chang -

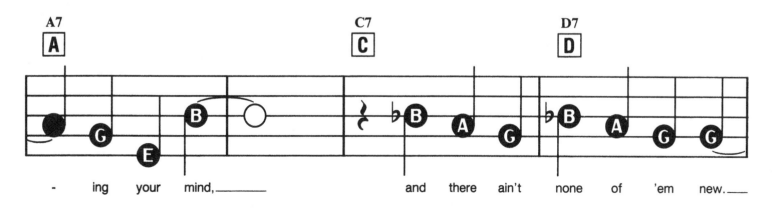

- ing your mind,_____ and there ain't none of 'em new._____

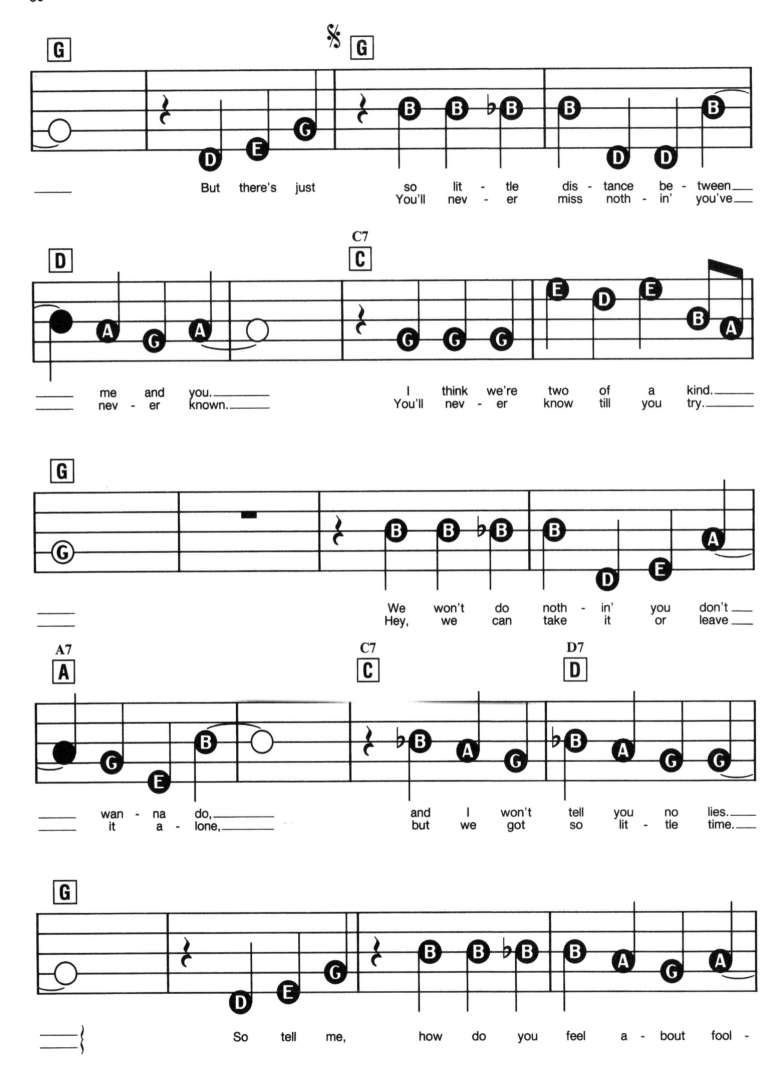

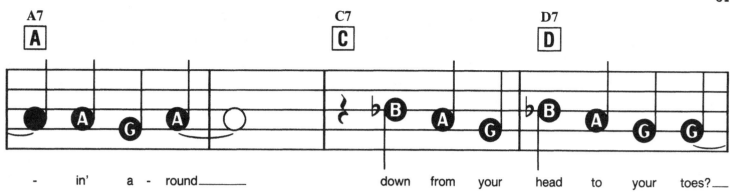

- in' a - round_____ down from your head to your toes?___

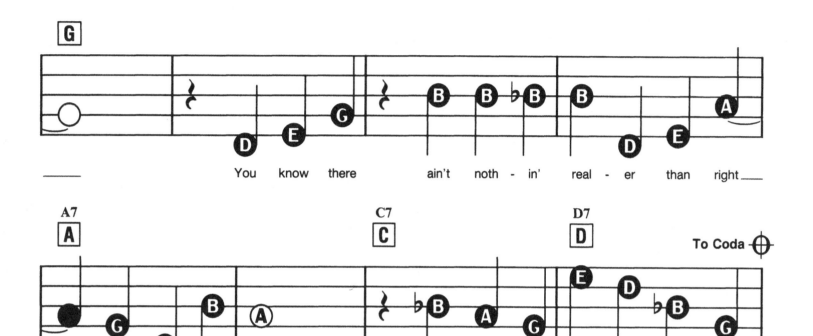

_____ You know there ain't noth - in' real - er than right___

_____ here and now,_____ and that's as far as it goes.___

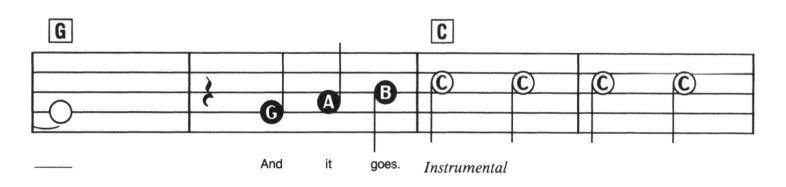

_____ And it goes. *Instrumental*

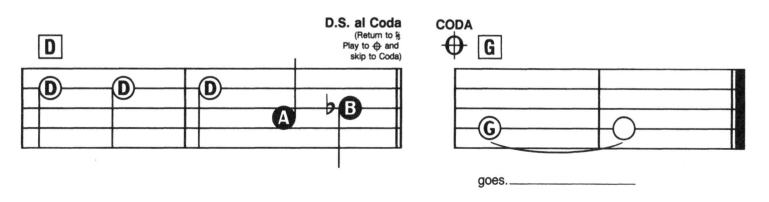

goes._____

Heaven And Hell

Registration 1
Rhythm: Waltz

Words and Music by
Willie Nelson

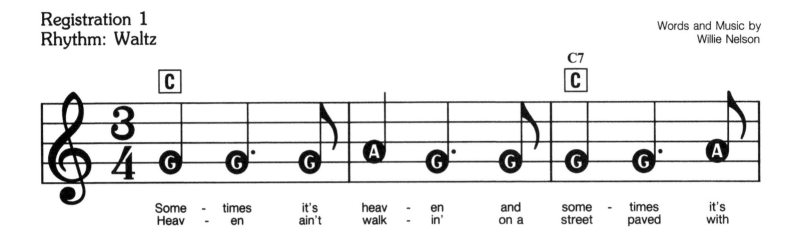

Some - times it's heav - en and some - times it's
Heav - en ain't walk - in' on a street paved with

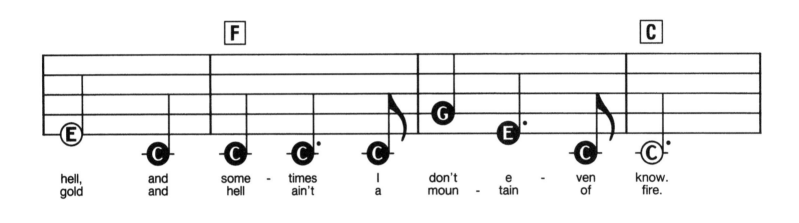

hell, and some - times I don't e - ven know.
gold and hell ain't a moun - tain of fire.

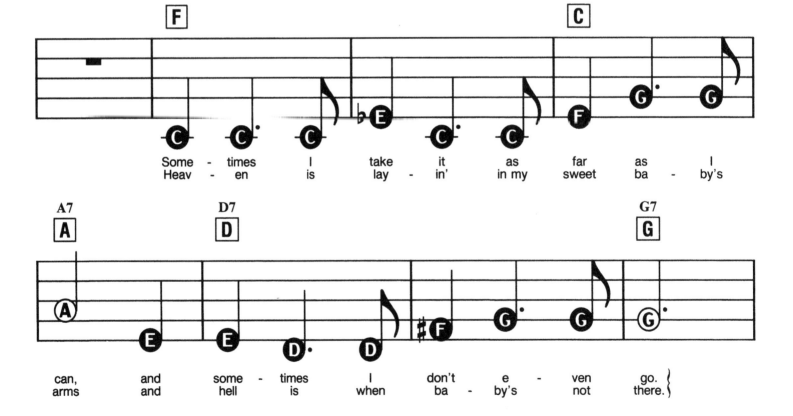

Some - times I take it as far as I
Heav - en is lay - in' in my sweet ba - by's

can, and some - times I don't e - ven go.
arms and hell is when ba - by's not there. {

33

Help Me Make It Through The Night

Registration 2
Rhythm: Country or Fox Trot

Words and Music by
Kris Kristofferson

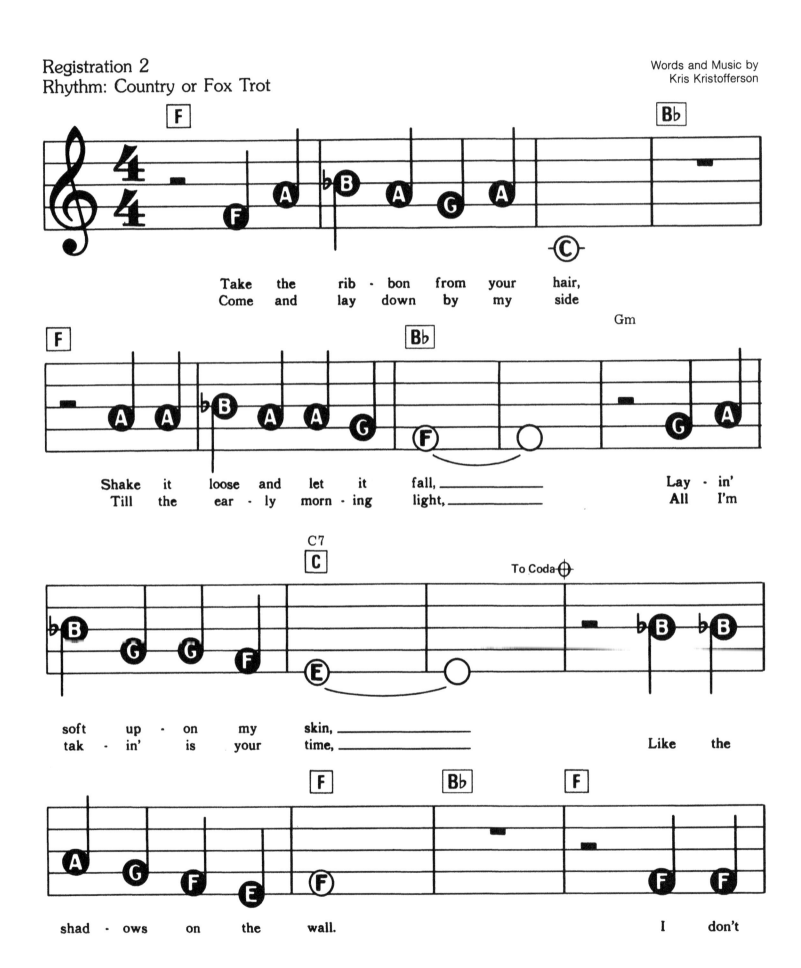

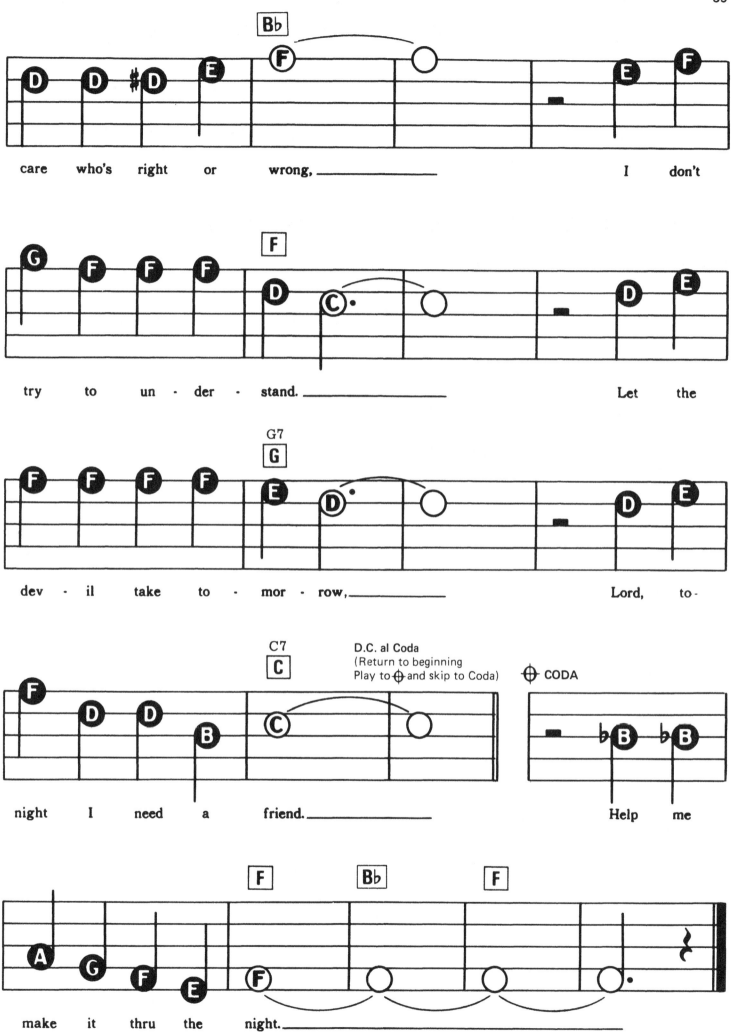

Loving Her Was Easier
(Than Anything I'll Ever Do Again)

Registration 1
Rhythm: Rock or Pop

Words and Music by
Kris Kristofferson

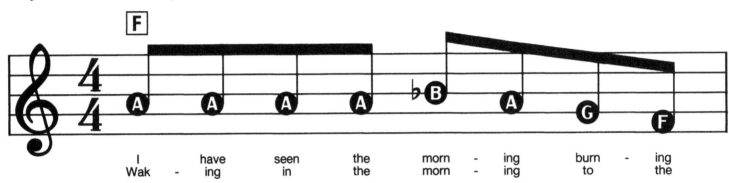

I have seen the morn - ing burn - ing
Wak - ing in the morn - ing to the

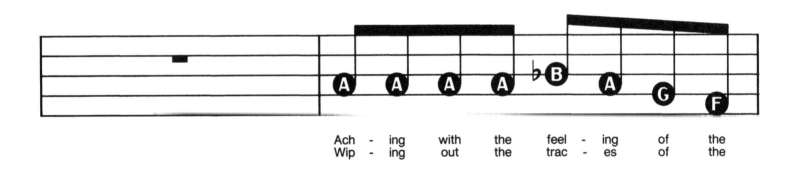

gold - en on the moun - tain in the skies.
feel - ing of her fin - gers on my skin.

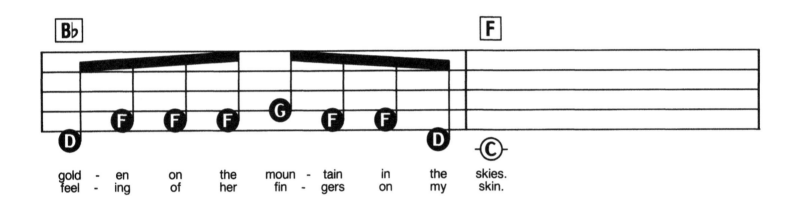

Ach - ing with the feel - ing of the
Wip - ing out the trac - es of the

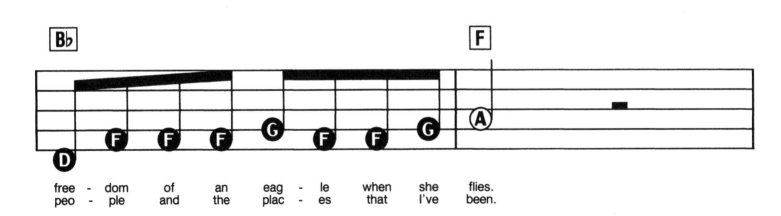

free - dom of an eag - le when she flies.
peo - ple and the plac - es that I've been.

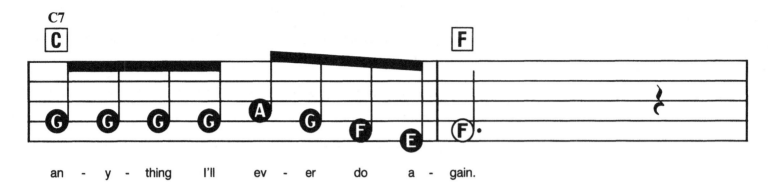

an - y - thing I'll ev - er do a - gain.

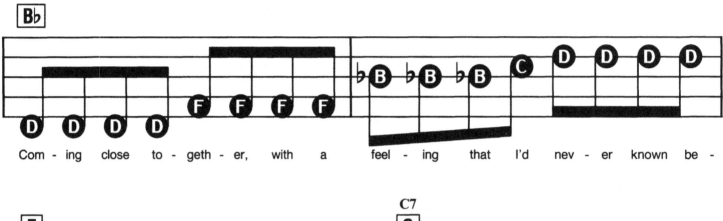

Com - ing close to - geth - er, with a feel - ing that I'd nev - er known be -

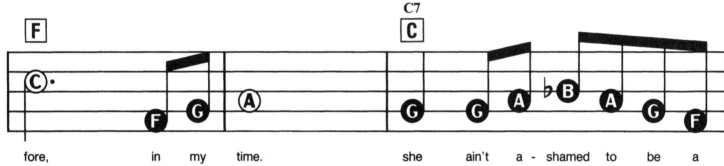

fore, in my time. she ain't a - shamed to be a

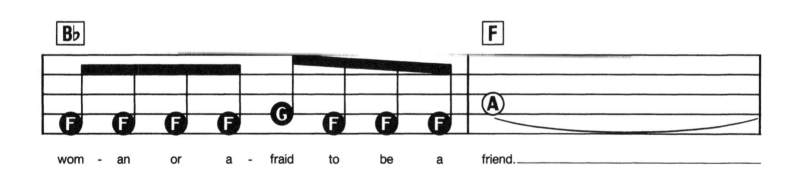

wom - an or a - fraid to be a friend._____

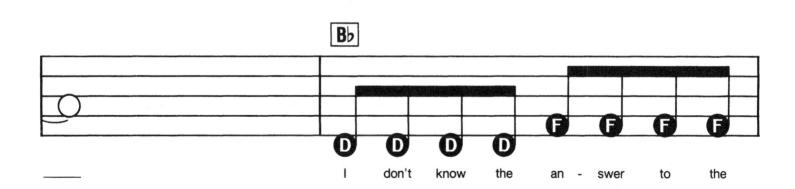

_____ I don't know the an - swer to the

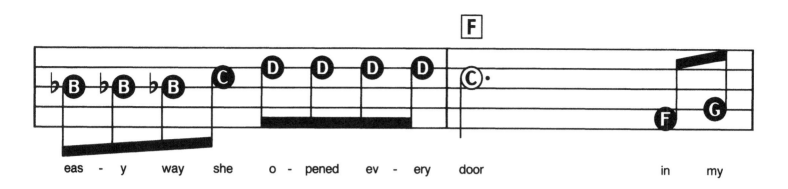

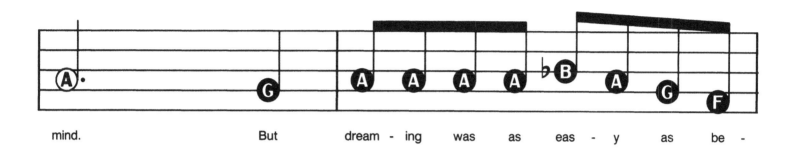

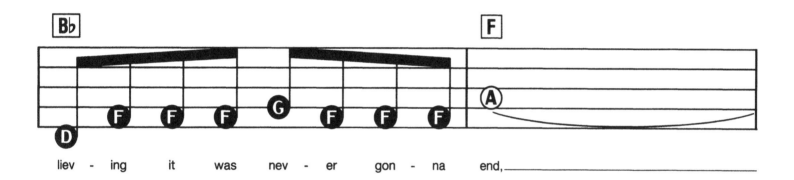

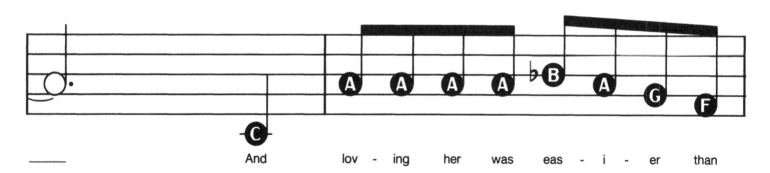

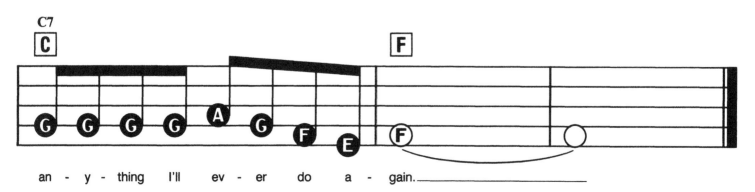

Make The World Go Away

Registration 10
Rhythm: Swing or Country

By Hank Cochran

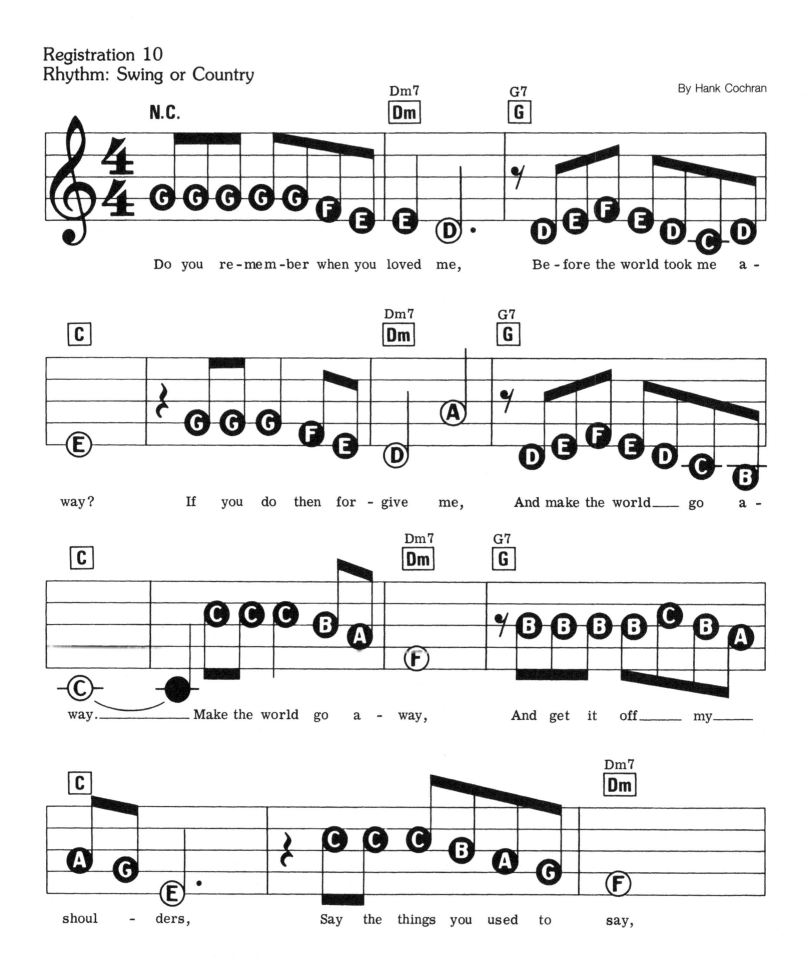

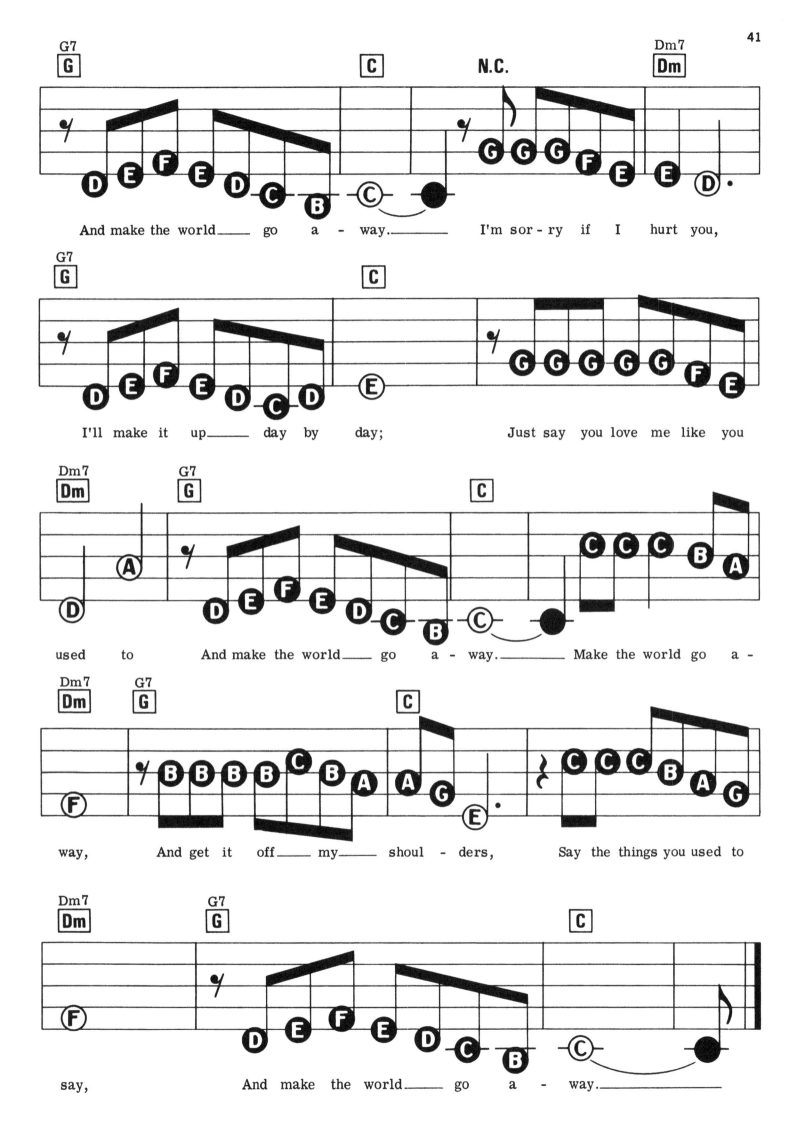

Mammas Don't Let Your Babies Grow Up To Be Cowboys

Registration 2
Rhythm: Waltz

Words and Music by
Ed Bruce and Patsy Bruce

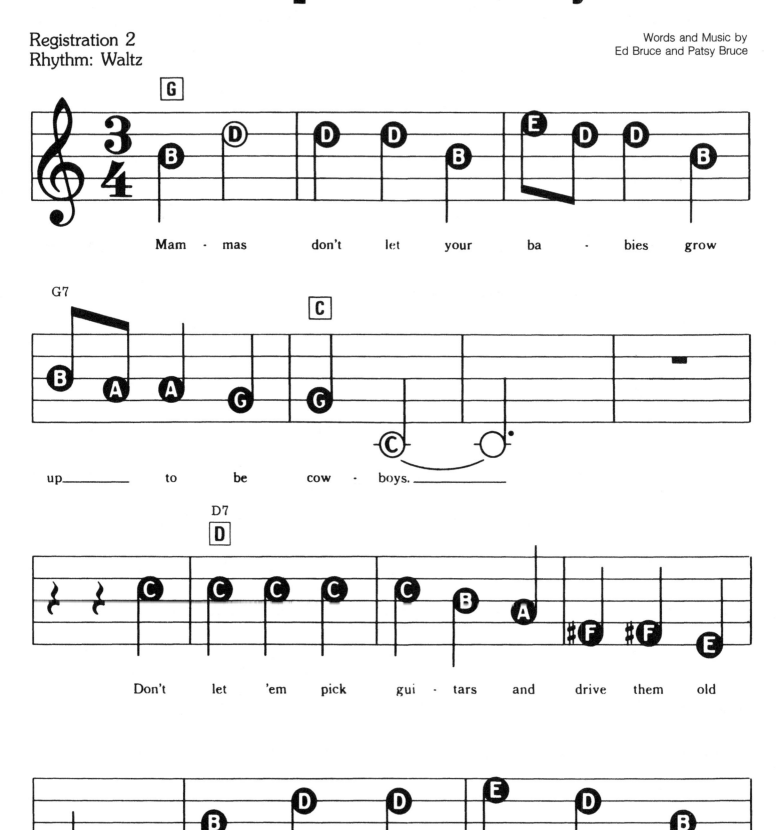

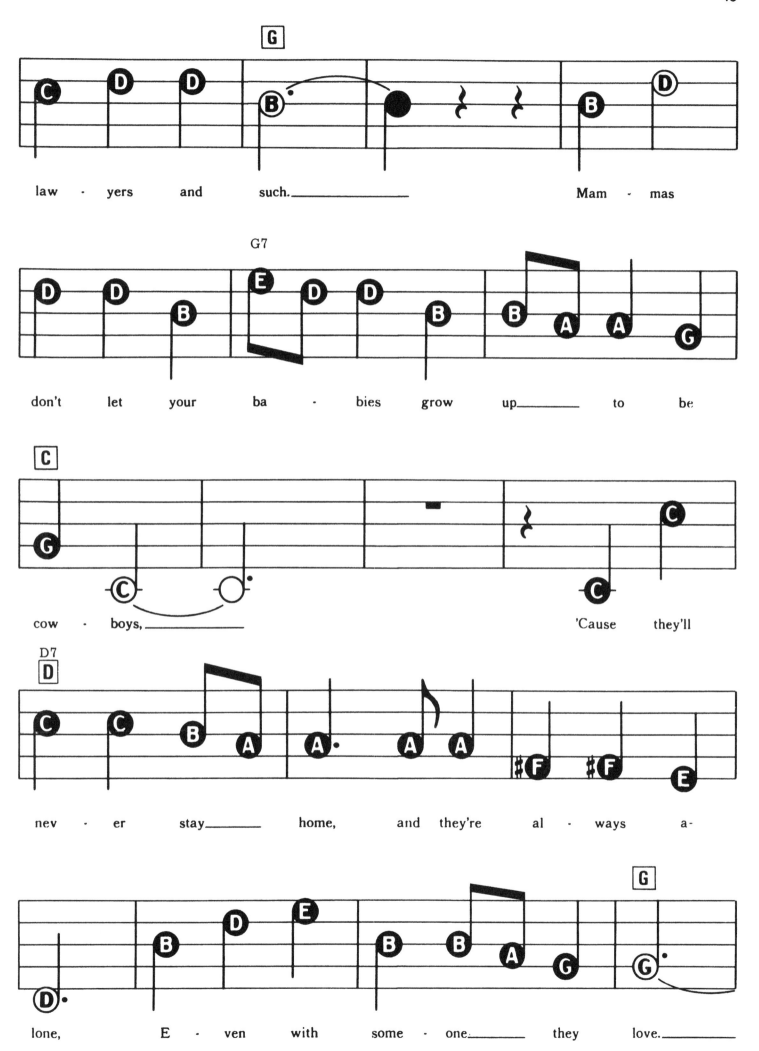

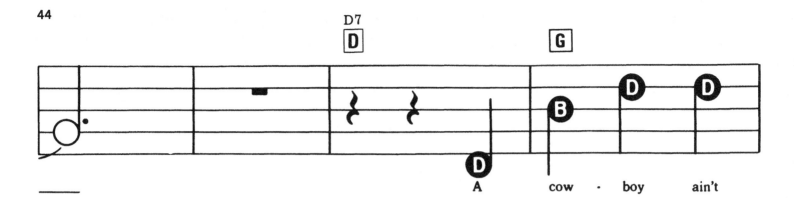

A cow - boy ain't

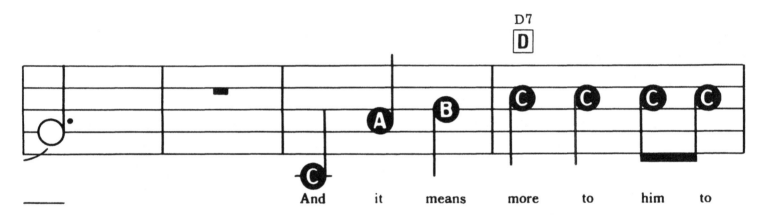

eas - y to love and he's hard - er____ to hold.____

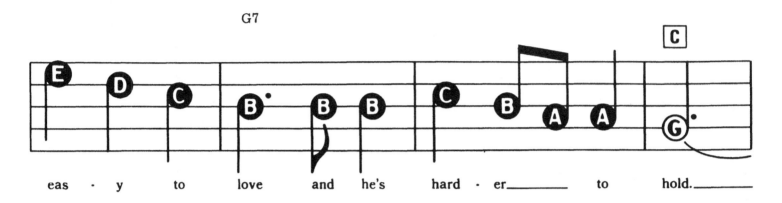

And it means more to him to

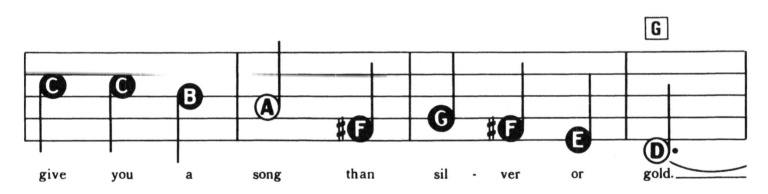

give you a song than sil - ver or gold.____

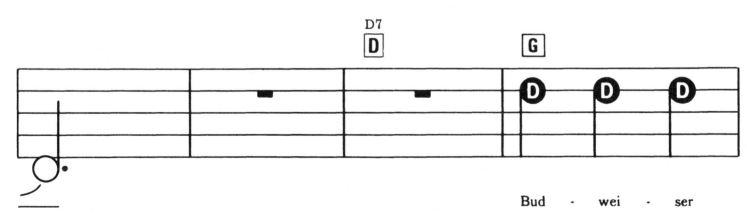

Bud - wei - ser

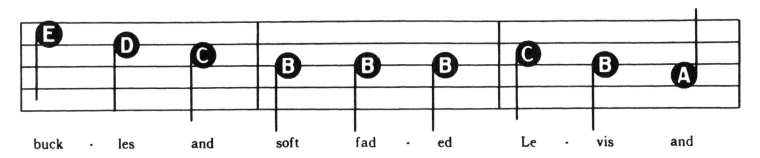

G7

buck - les and soft fad - ed Le - vis and

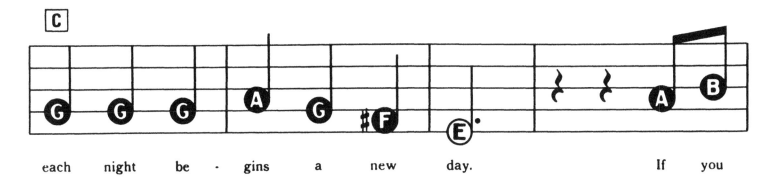

C

each night be - gins a new day. If you

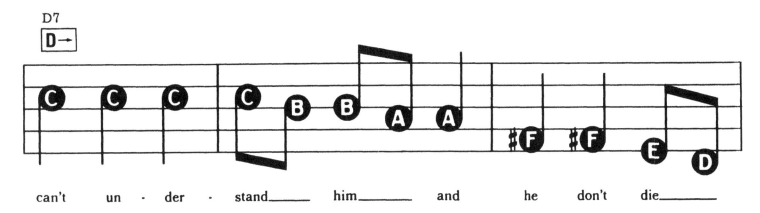

D7
D→

can't un - der - stand____ him____ and he don't die____

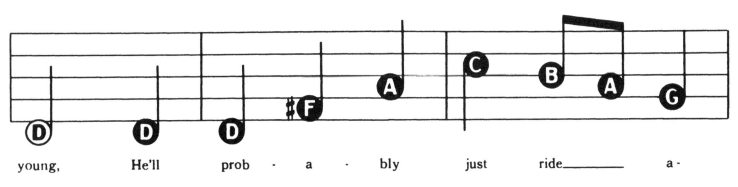

young, He'll prob - a - bly just ride____ a -

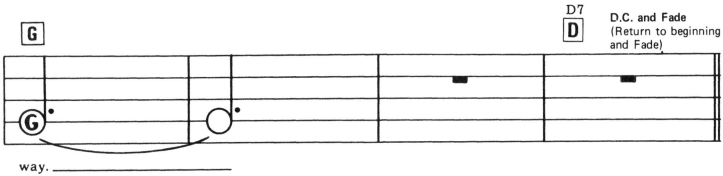

G

D7
D

D.C. and Fade
(Return to beginning
and Fade)

way. ____

My Heroes Have Always Been Cowboys

Registration 9
Rhythm: Waltz

Words and Music by
Sharon Vaughn

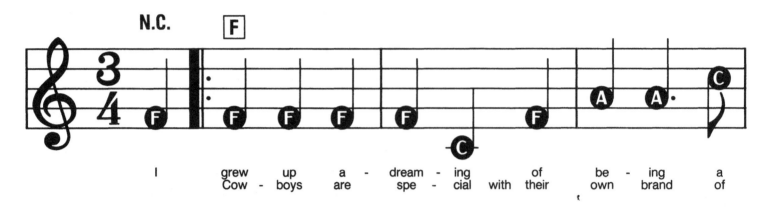

I grew up a - dream - ing of be - ing a
Cow - boys are spe - cial with their own brand of

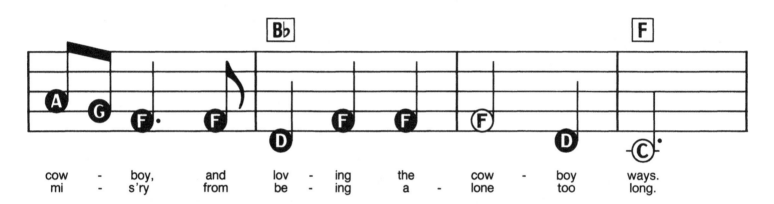

cow - boy, and lov - ing the cow - boy ways.
mi - s'ry from be - ing a - lone too long.

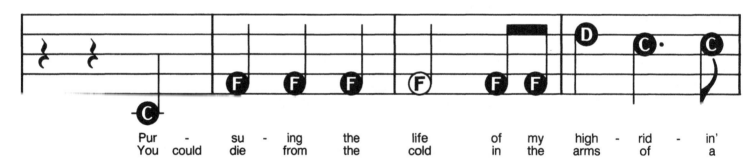

Pur - su - ing the life of my high - rid - in'
You could die from the cold in the arms of a

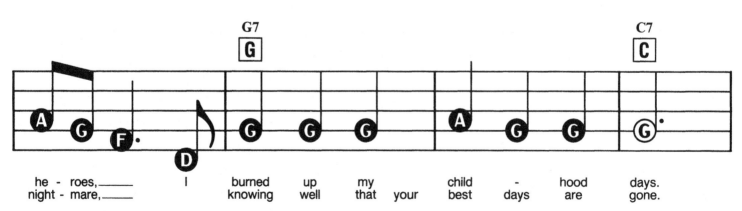

he - roes, _____ I burned up my child - hood days.
night - mare, _____ knowing well that your best days are gone.

47

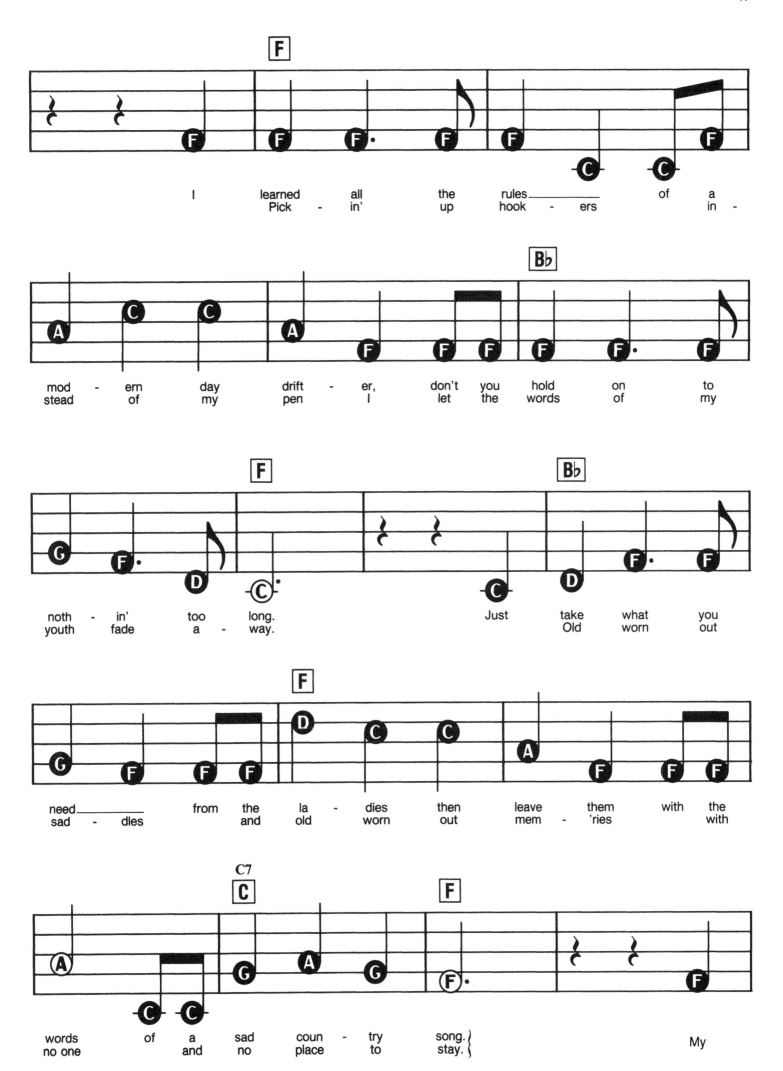

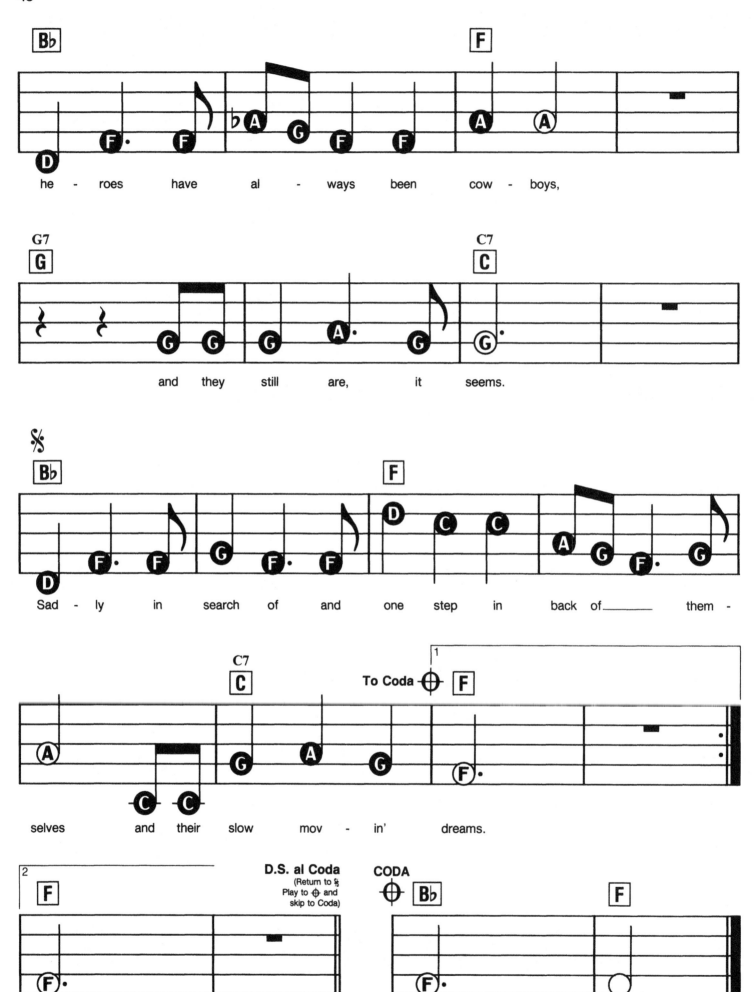

Reasons To Quit

Registration 10
Rhythm: Country or Shuffle

Words and Music by
Merle Haggard

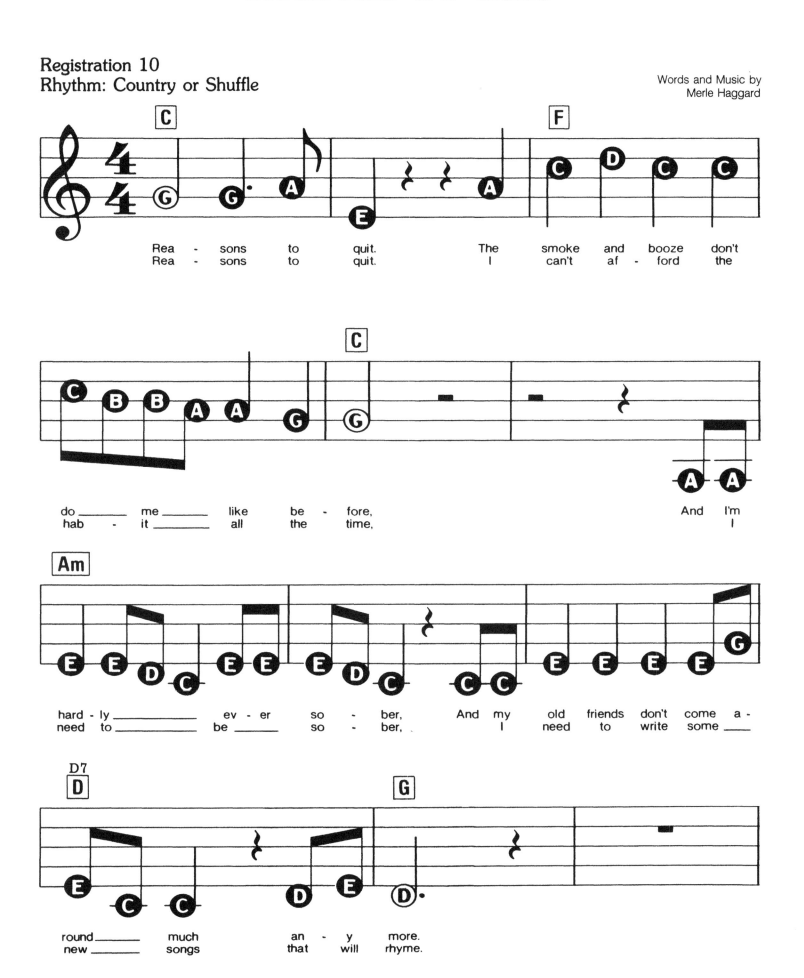

Rea - sons to quit. The smoke and booze don't
Rea - sons to quit. I can't af - ford the

do ____ me ____ like be - fore, And I'm
hab - it ____ all the time, I

hard - ly ____ ev - er so - ber, And my old friends don't come a -
need to ____ be ____ so - ber, I need to write some ____

round ____ much an - y more.
new ____ songs that will rhyme.

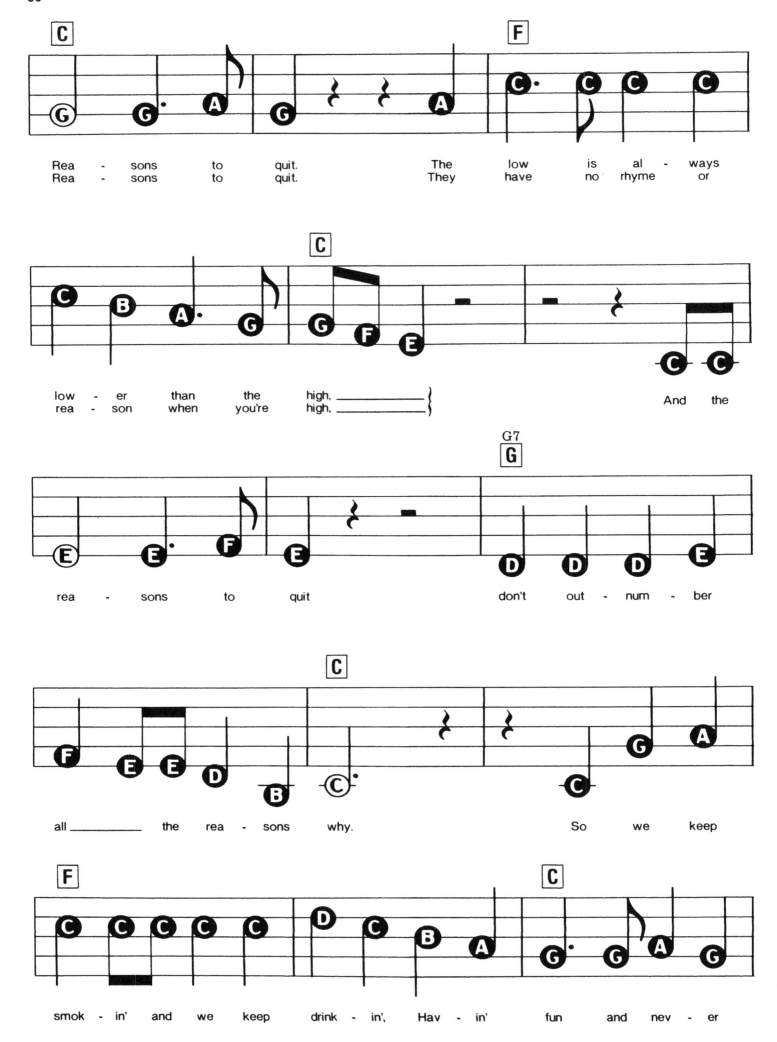

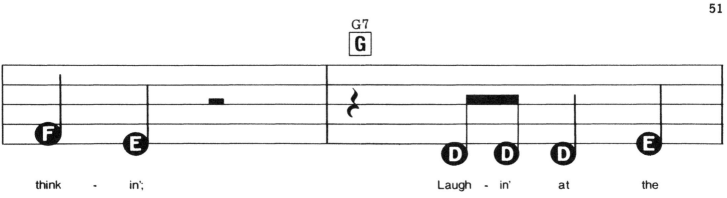

think - in'; Laugh - in' at the

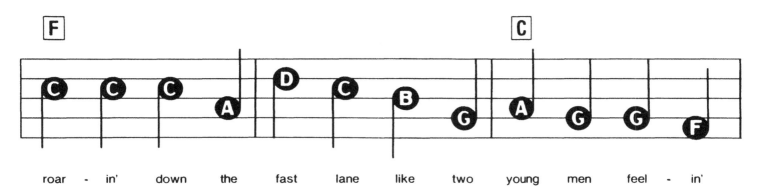

price - tags____ that we pay. And we keep

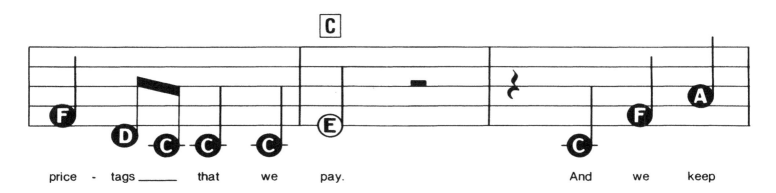

roar - in' down the fast lane like two young men feel - in'

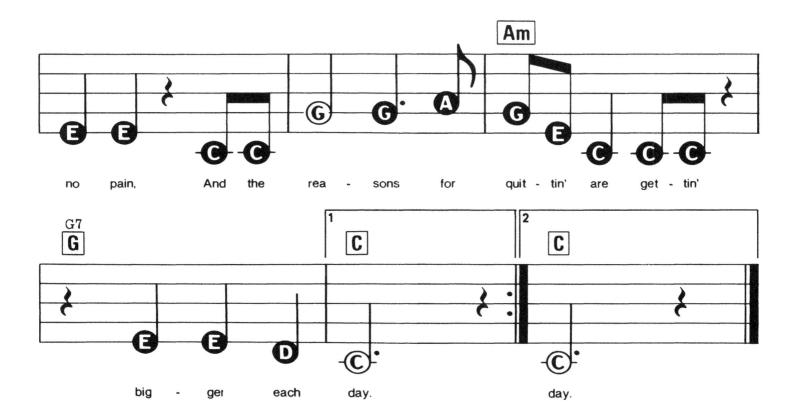

no pain, And the rea - sons for quit - tin' are get - tin'

big - ger each day. day.

On The Road Again

Registration 7
Rhythm: Swing

Words and Music by
Willie Nelson

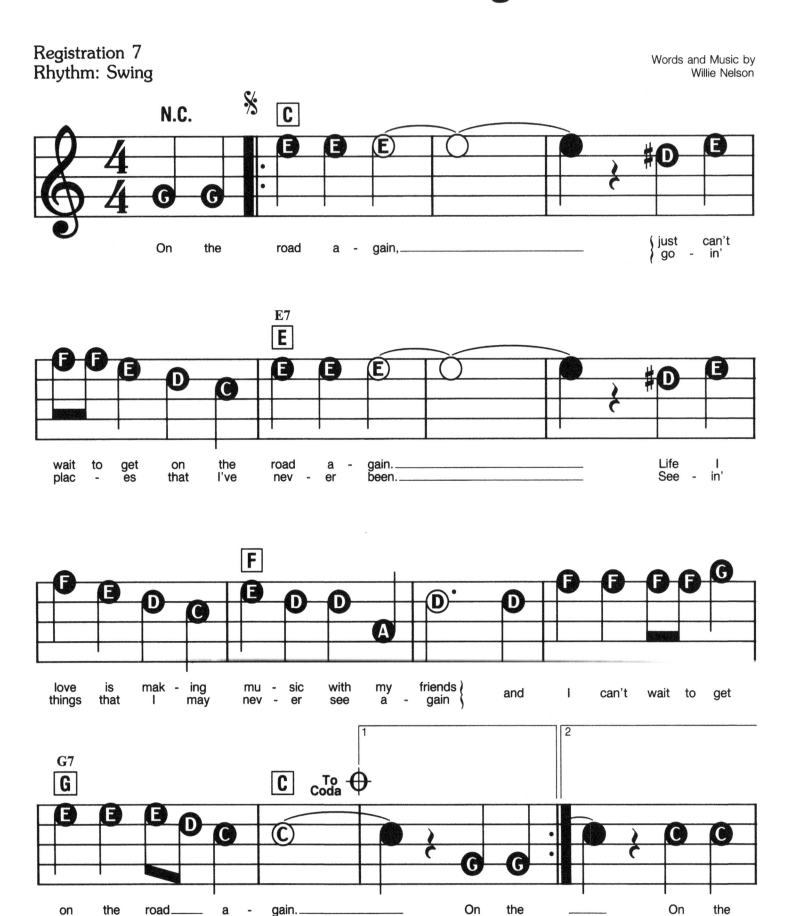

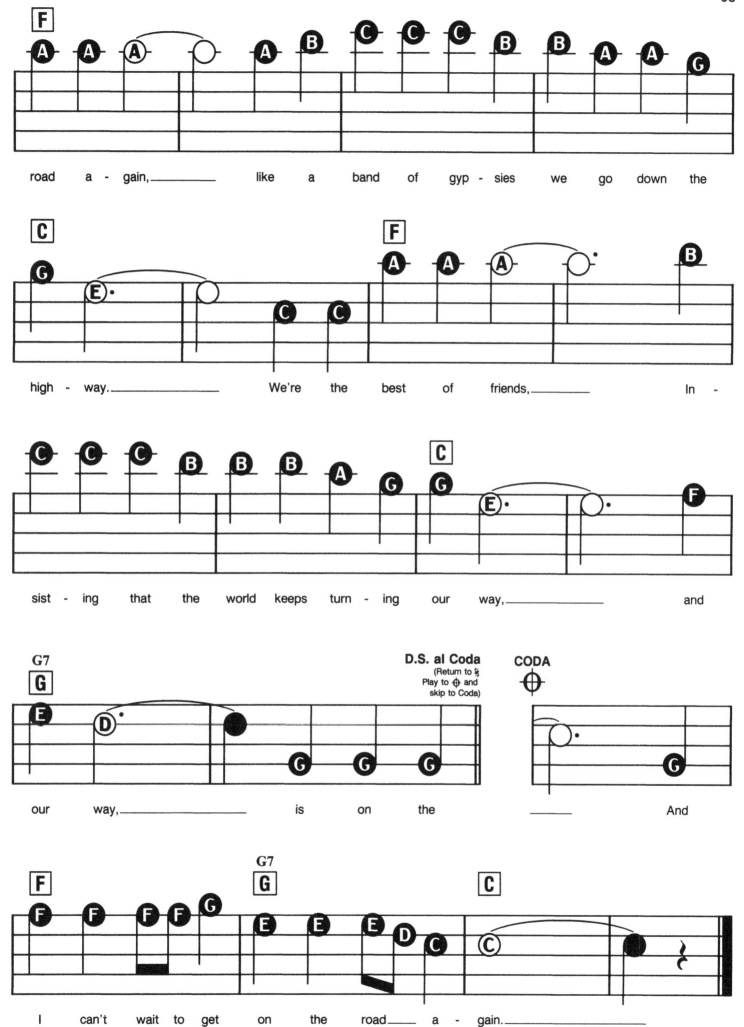

Seven Spanish Angels

Registration 4
Rhythm: Latin

Words and Music by
Eddie Setser and Troy Seals

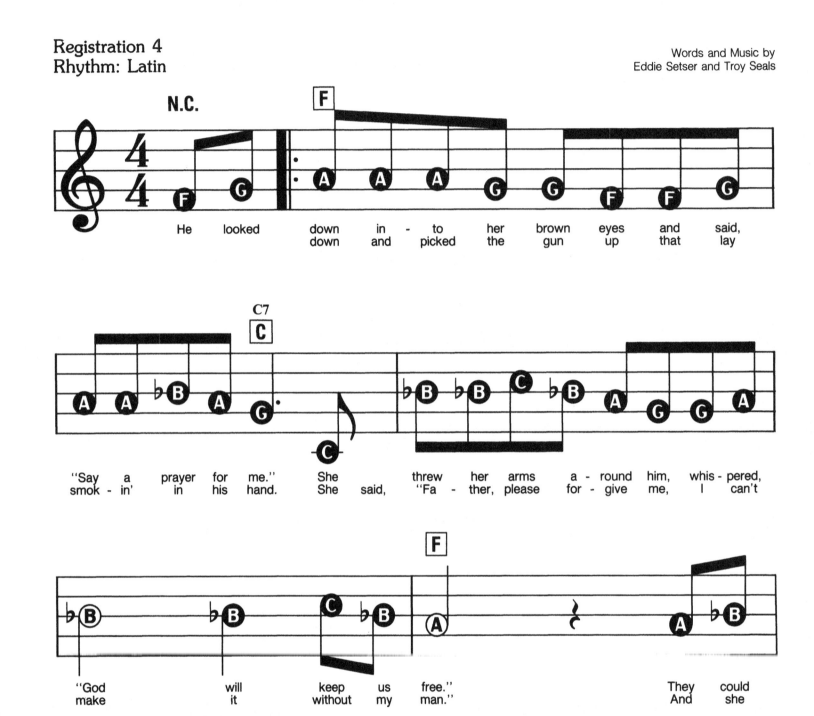

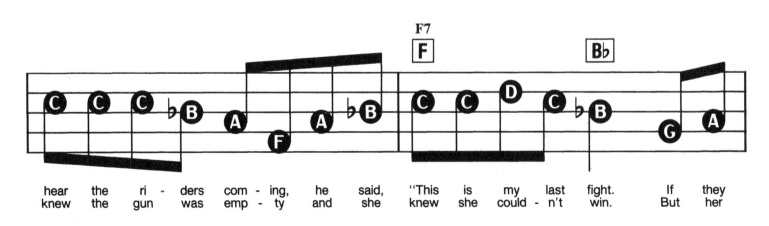

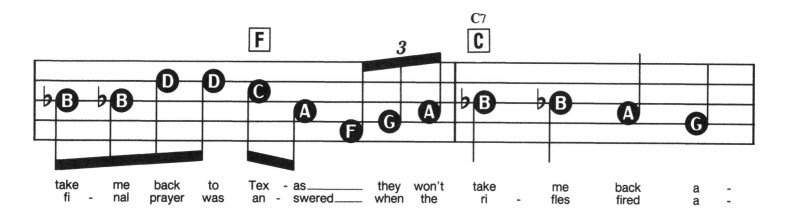

take me back to Tex - as_____ they won't take me back a -
fi - nal prayer was an - swered_____ when the ri - fles fired a -

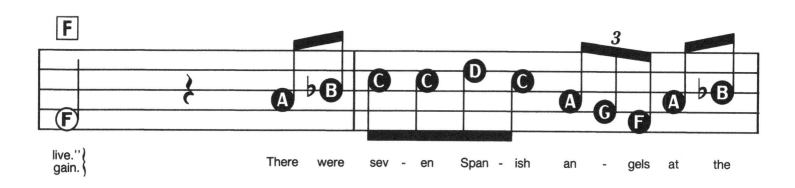

live."}
gain.}

There were sev - en Span - ish an - gels at the

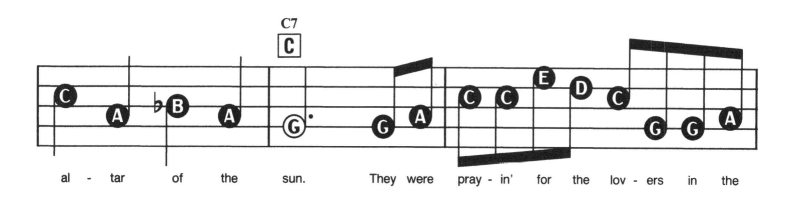

al - tar of the sun. They were pray - in' for the lov - ers in the

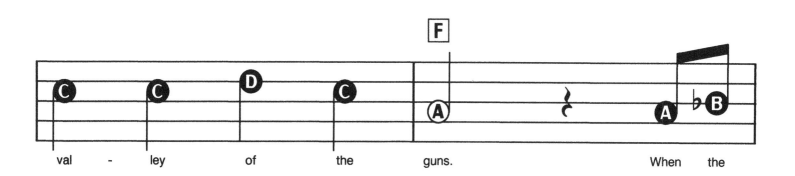

val - ley of the guns. When the

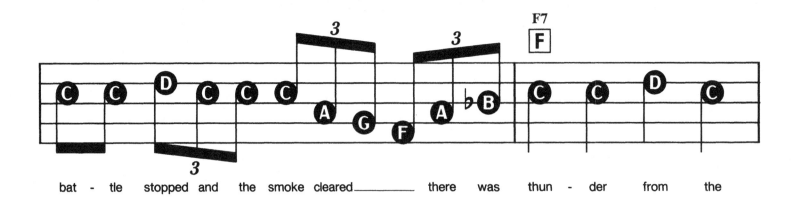

bat - tle stopped and the smoke cleared_____ there was thun - der from the

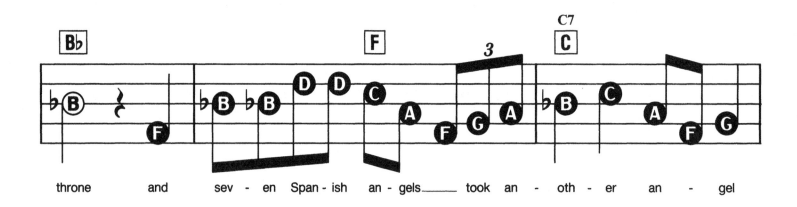

throne and sev - en Span - ish an - gels_____ took an - oth - er an - gel

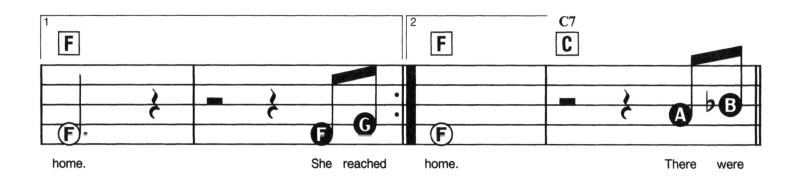

home. She reached home. There were

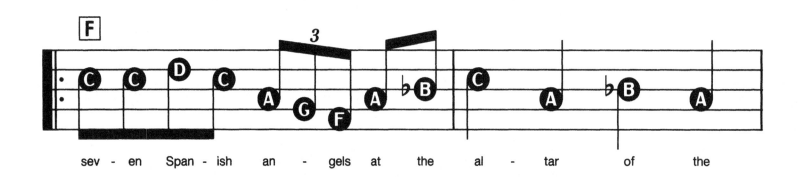

sev - en Span - ish an - gels at the al - tar of the

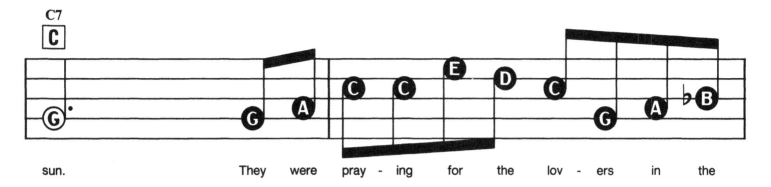

sun.   They   were   pray - ing   for   the   lov - ers   in   the

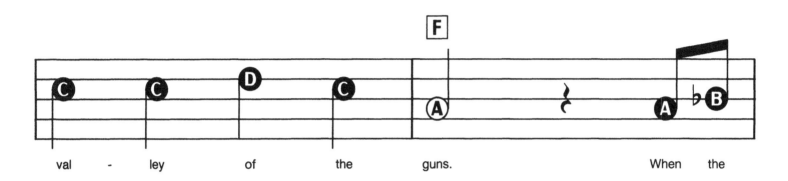

val - ley   of   the   guns.   When   the

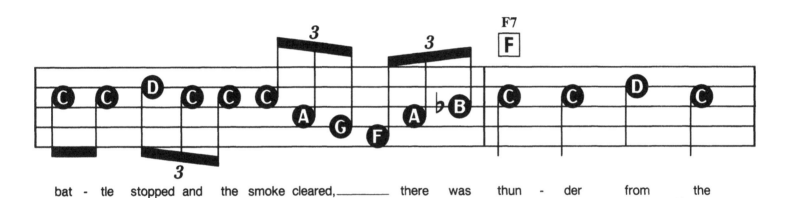

bat - tle stopped and the smoke cleared,_____ there was thun - der from the

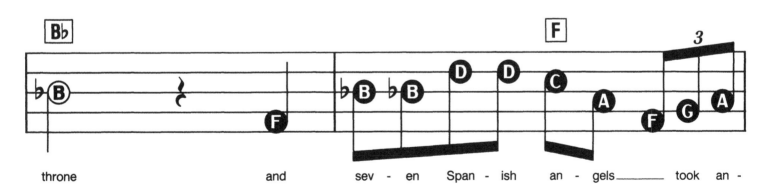

throne   and   sev - en Span - ish an - gels_____ took an -

Repeat and Fade

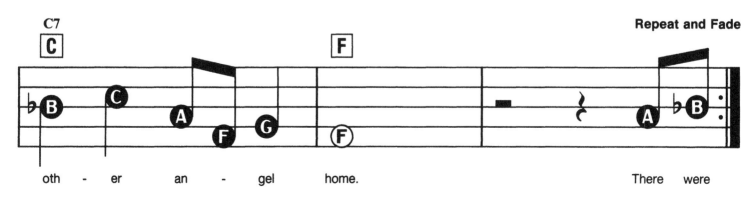

oth - er an - gel home.   There were

So You Think You're A Cowboy

Registration 2
Rhythm: Waltz

Words and Music by
Hank Cochran and Willie Nelson

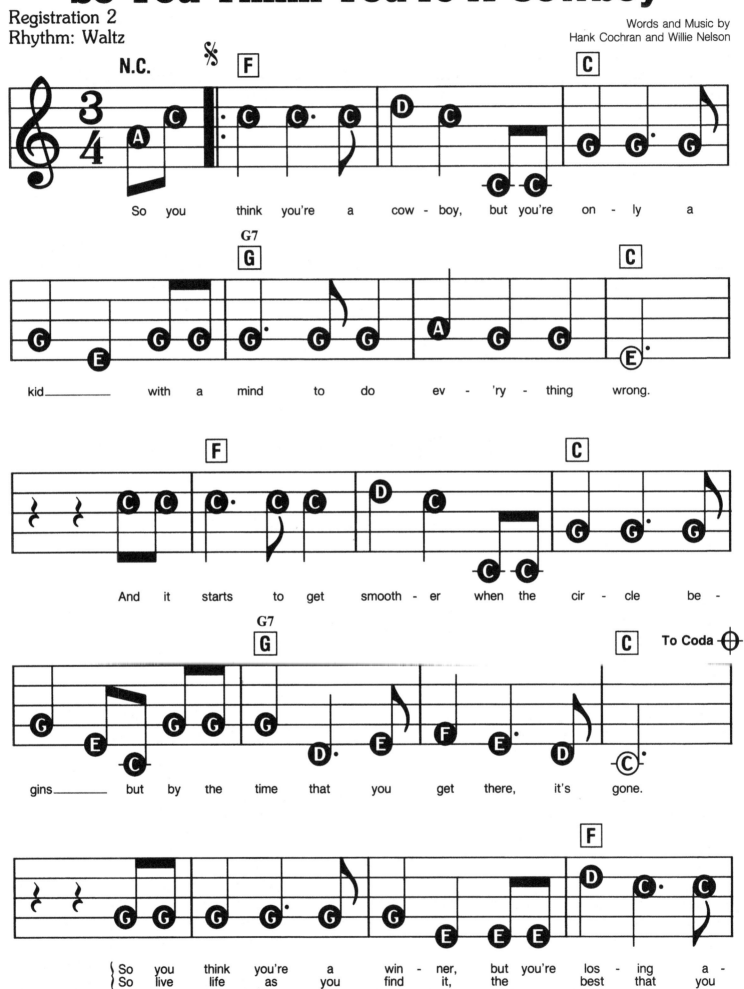

Take It To The Limit

Registration 3
Rhythm: Waltz

Words and Music by Randy Meisner,
Don Henley and Glenn Frey

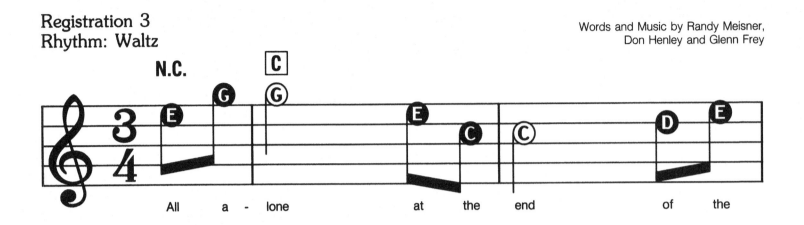

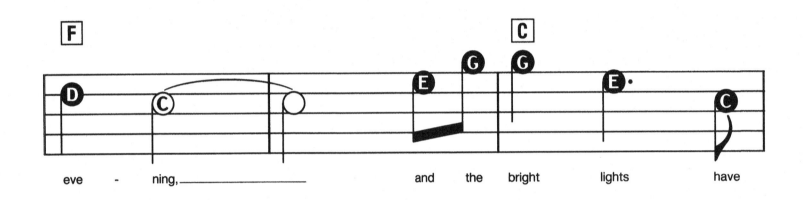

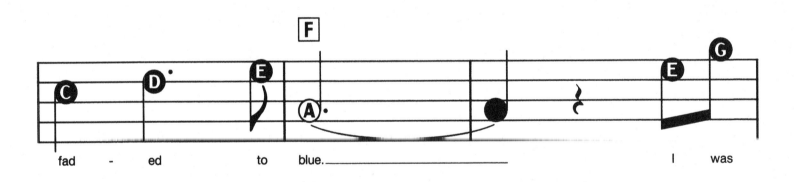

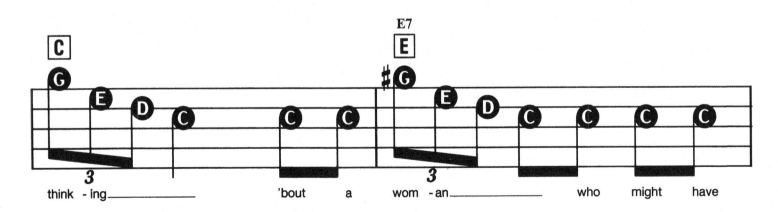

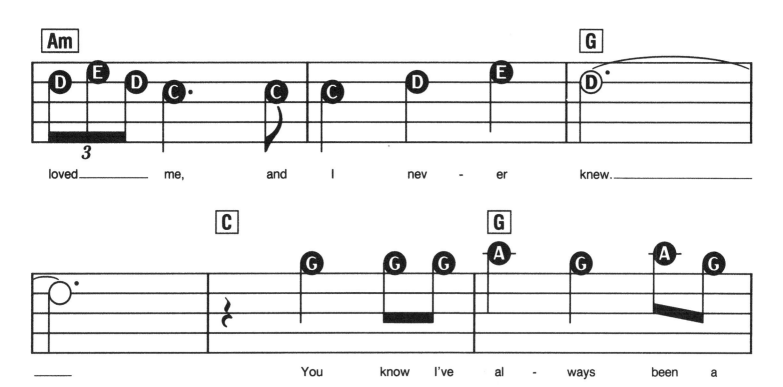

loved_____ me, and I nev - er knew._____

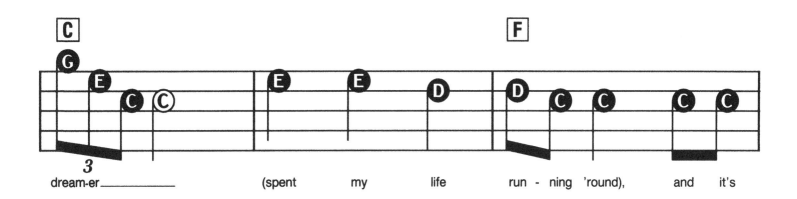

_____ You know I've al - ways been a

dream-er_____ (spent my life run - ning 'round), and it's

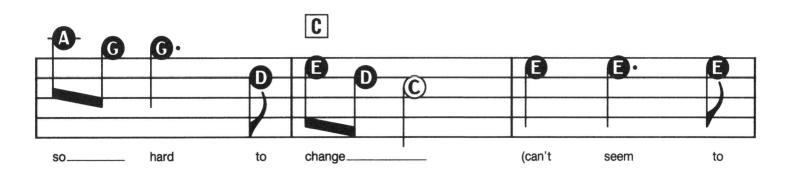

so_____ hard to change_____ (can't seem to

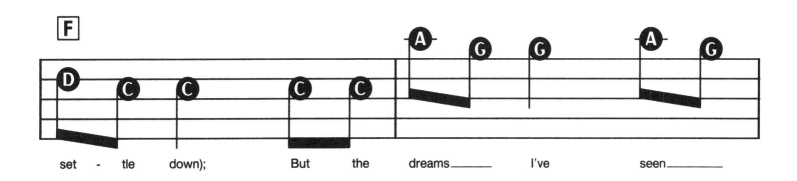

set - tle down); But the dreams_____ I've seen_____

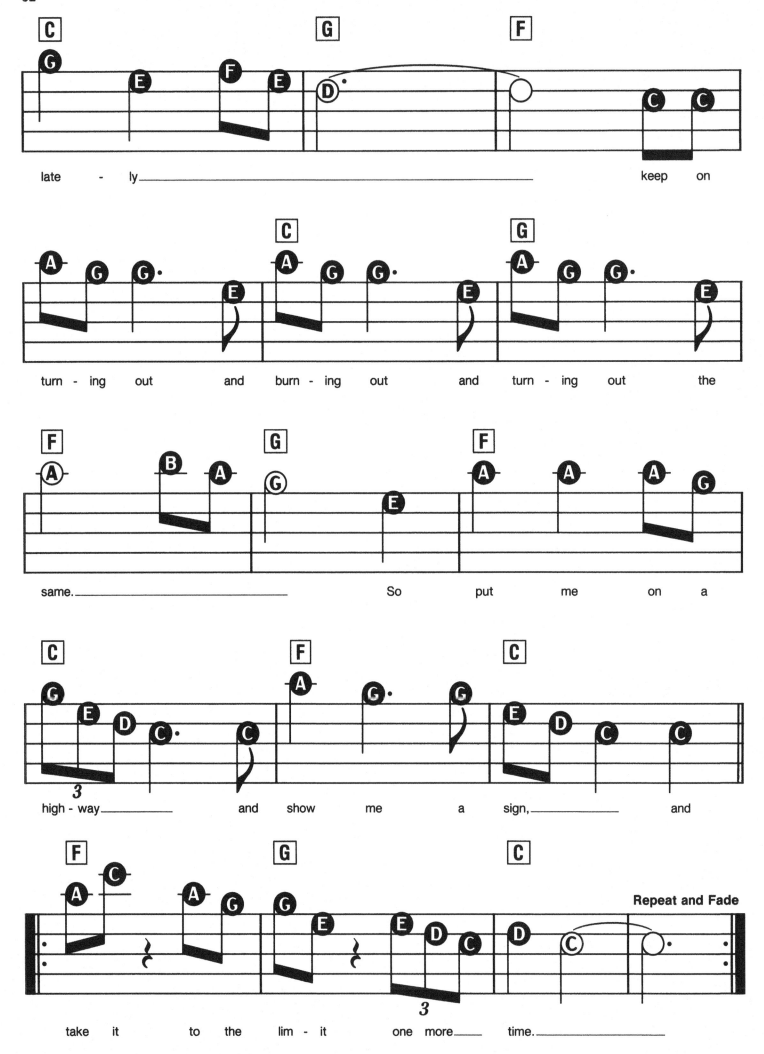

You Show Me Yours
(And I'll Show You Mine)

Registration 7
Rhythm: Waltz

Words and Music by
Kris Kristofferson

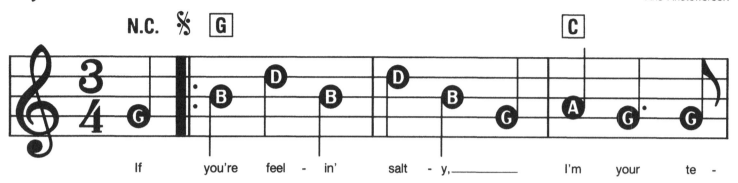

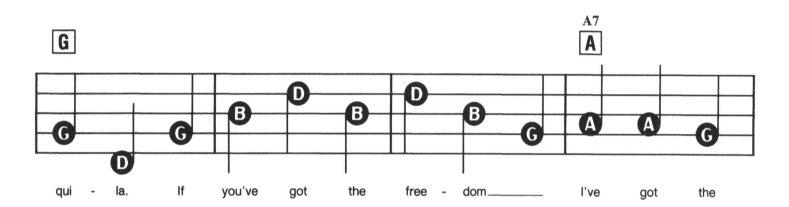

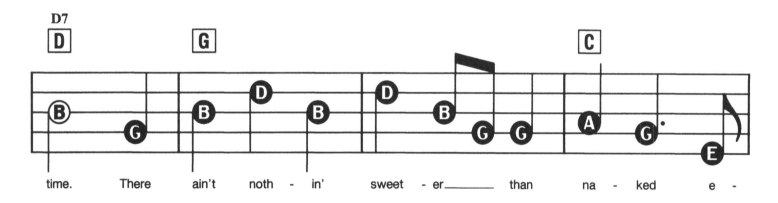

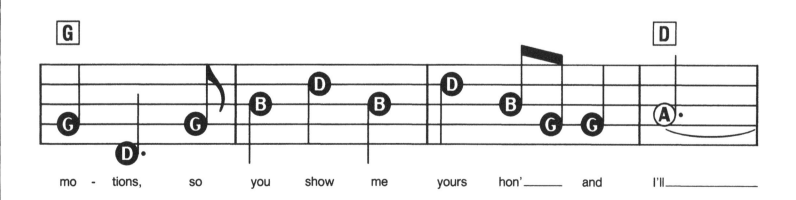

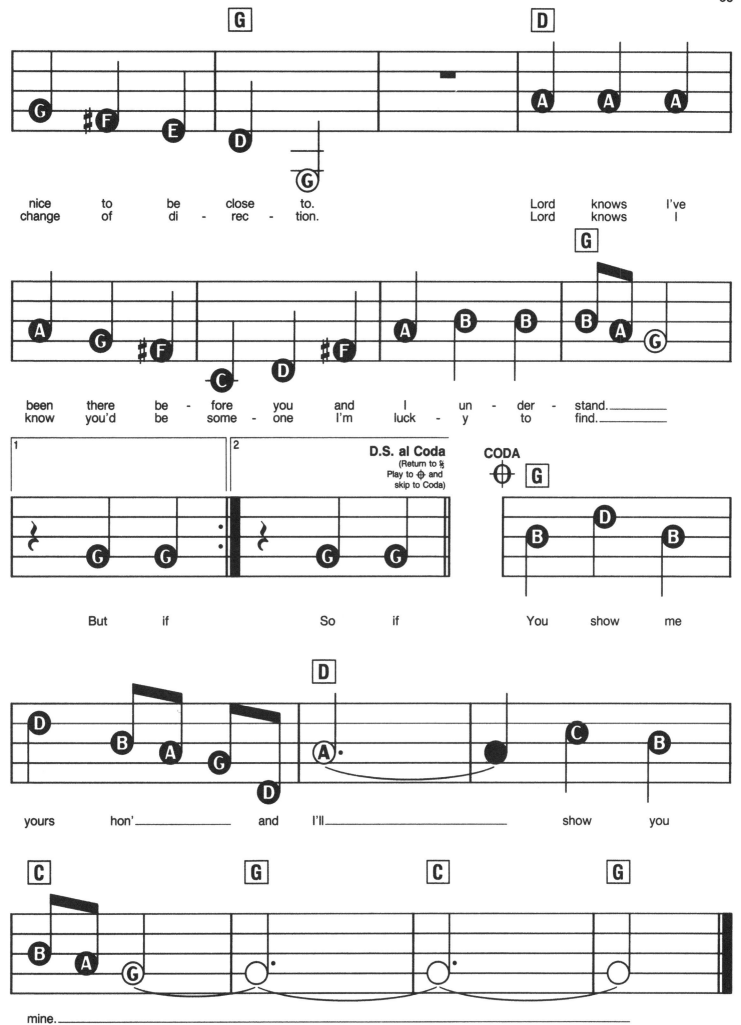

nice   to   be   close   to.   Lord   knows   I've
change   of   di - rec -   tion.   Lord   knows   I

been   there   be - fore   you   and   I   un - der - stand._____
know   you'd   be   some - one   I'm   luck - y   to   find._____

But   if   So   if

You   show   me

yours   hon'_____   and   I'll_____   show   you

mine._____

To All The Girls I've Loved Before

Registration 5
Rhythm: Rock

Lyric by Hal David
Music by Albert Hammond

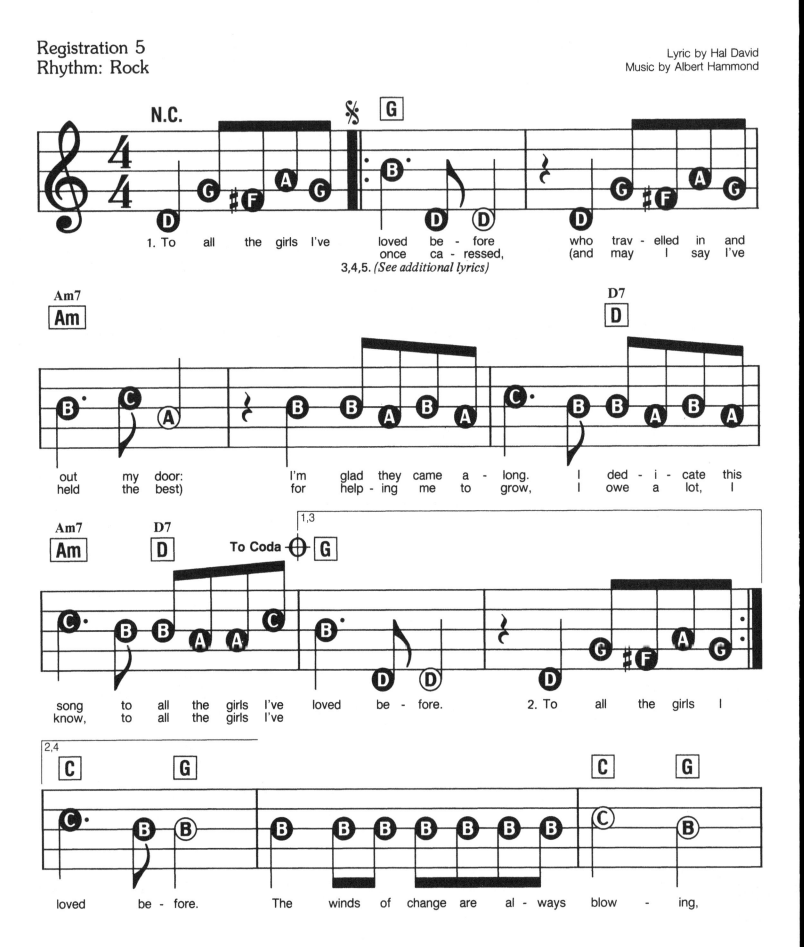

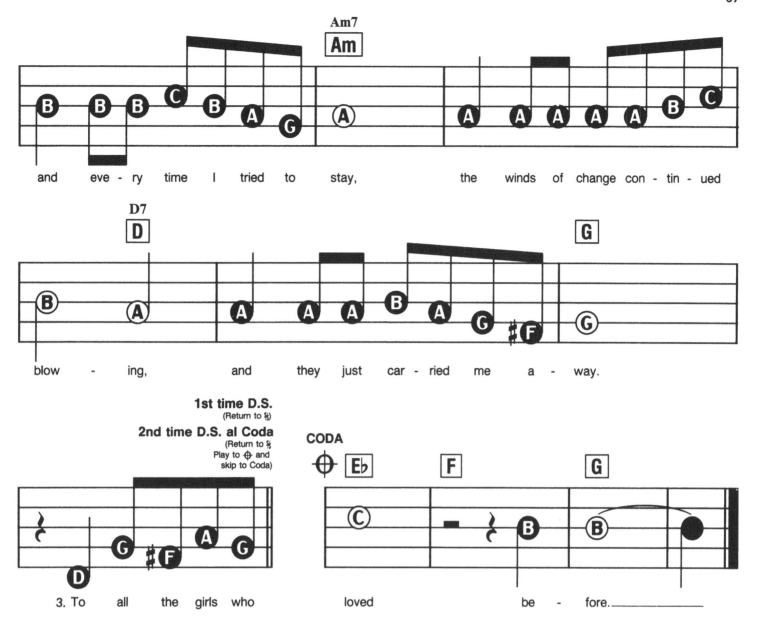

Additional Lyrics

3. To all the girls who shared my life,
Who now are someone else's wife;
I'm glad they came along
I dedicate this song
To all the girls I've loved before.

4. To all the girls who cared for me,
Who filled my nights with ecstasy;
They live within my heart,
I'll always be a part
Of all the girls I've loved before.

5. To all the girls we've loved before,
Who travelled in and out our door;
We're glad they came along,
We dedicate this song
To all the girls we've loved before.

Without A Song

Registration 2
Rhythm: Slow Rock or Ballad

Words by William Rose and Edward Eliscu
Music by Vincent Youmans

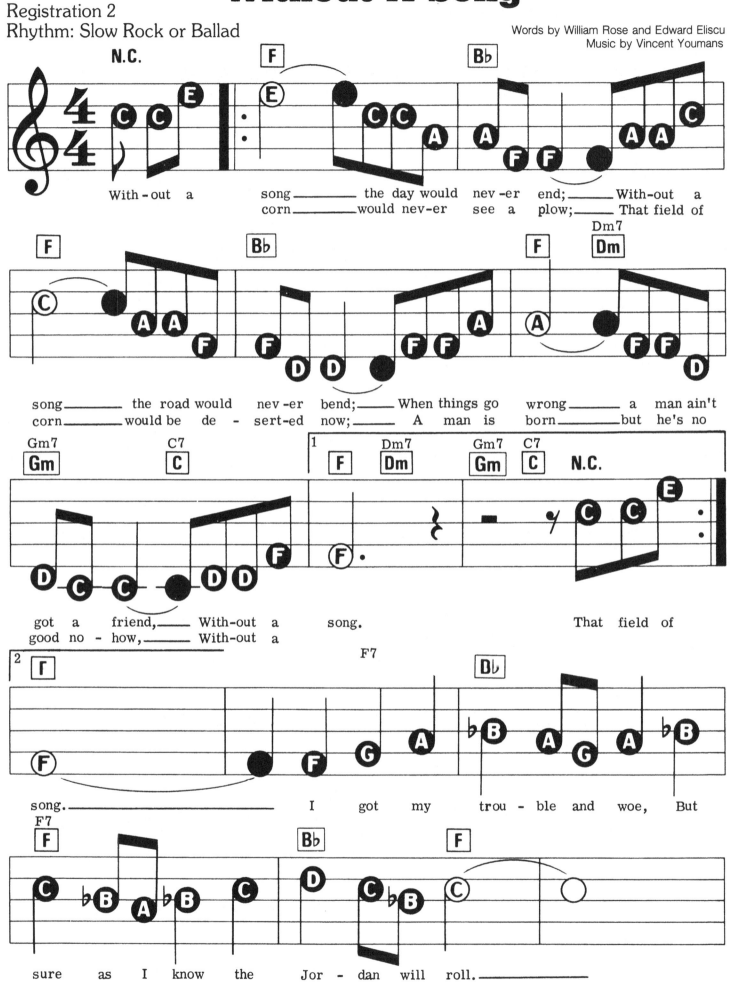

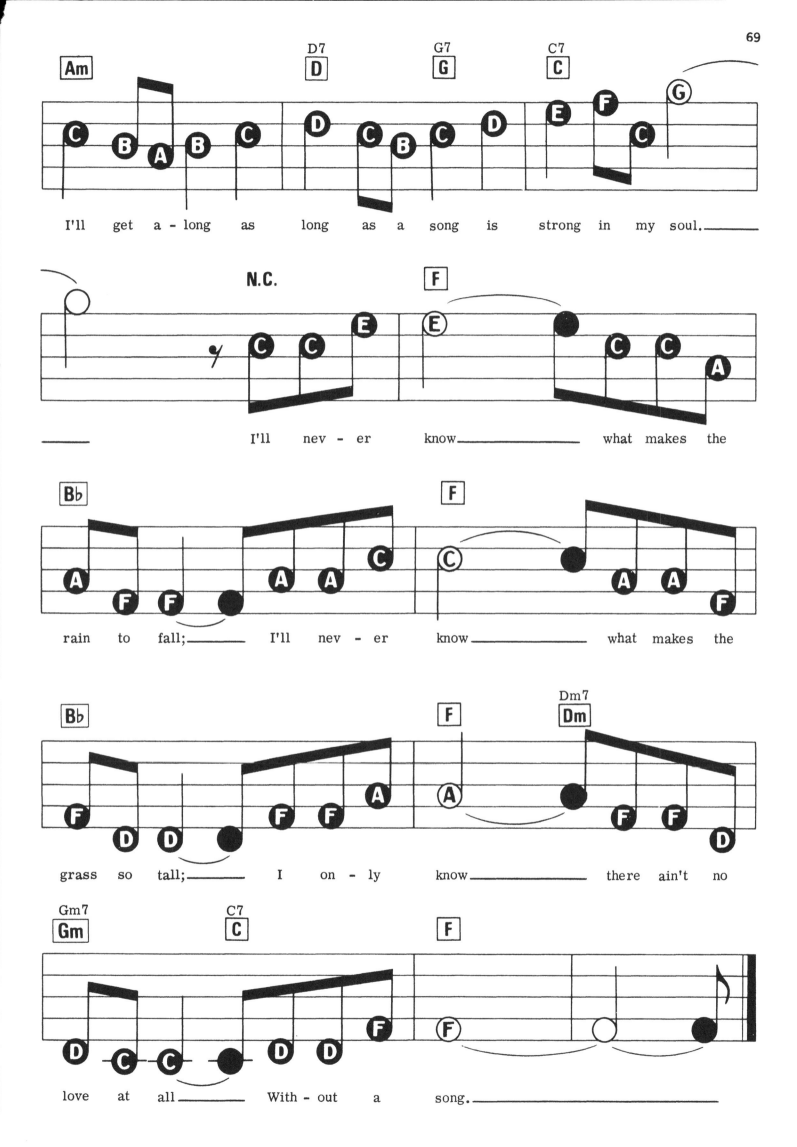

Workin' Man Blues

Registration 5
Rhythm: Blues or Country

Words and Music by
Merle Haggard

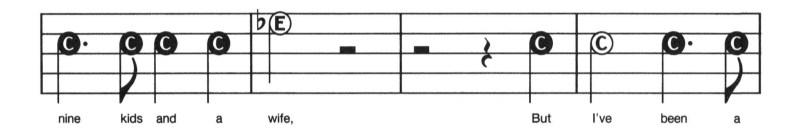

1. It's a big job just get - tin' by with
2-4. *(See additional lyrics)*

nine kids and a wife, But I've been a

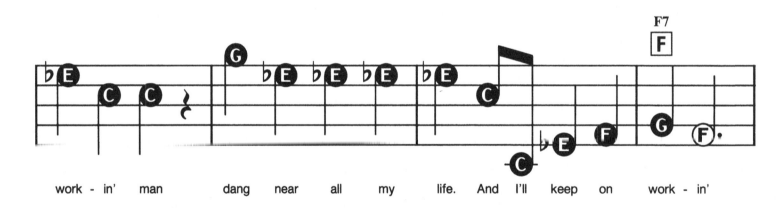

work - in' man dang near all my life. And I'll keep on work - in'

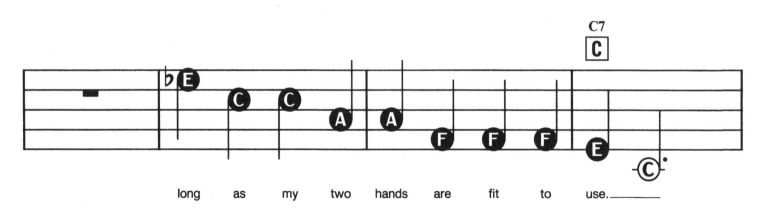

long as my two hands are fit to use._____

I'll drink my beer in a

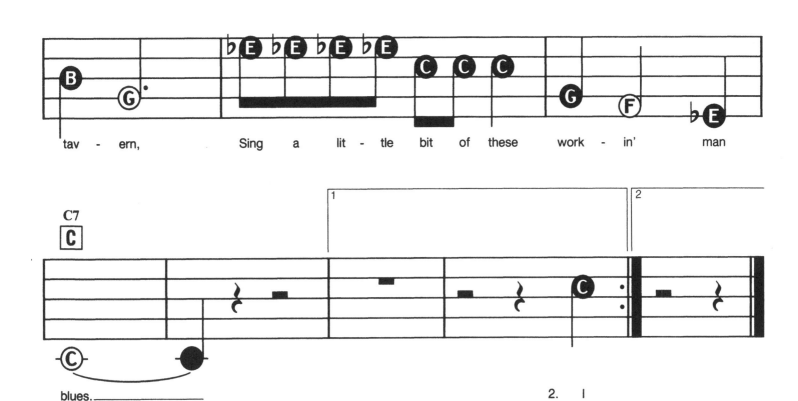

tav - ern, Sing a lit - tle bit of these work - in' man

blues._____ 2. I

Additional Lyrics

2. I keep my nose on the grindstone, work hard everyday.
   I might get a little tired on the weekend, after I draw my pay.
   I'll go back workin', come Monday morning I'm right back with the crew.
   And I drink a little beer that evening,
      Sing a little bit of these workin' man blues.

3. Sometimes I think about leaving, do a little bumming around.
   I want to throw my bills out the window, catch a train to another town.
   I'll go back workin', gotta buy my kids a brand new pair of shoes.
   I drink a little beer in a tavern,
      Cry a little bit of these workin' man blues.

4. Well, Hey! Hey! The workin' man, the workin' man like me
   I ain't never been on welfare, that's one place I won't be.
   I'll be workin', long as my two hands are fit to use.
   I'll drink my beer in a tavern
      Sing a little bit of these workin' man blues.

Registration Guide

- Match the Registration number on the song to the corresponding numbered category below. Select and activate an instrumental sound available on your instrument.

- Choose an automatic rhythm appropriate to the mood and style of the song. (Consult your Owner's Guide for proper operation of automatic rhythm features.)

- Adjust the tempo and volume controls to comfortable settings.

Registration

1	Mellow	Flutes, Clarinet, Oboe, Flugel Horn, Trombone, French Horn, Organ Flutes
2	Ensemble	Brass Section, Sax Section, Wind Ensemble, Full Organ, Theater Organ
3	Strings	Violin, Viola, Cello, Fiddle, String Ensemble, Pizzicato, Organ Strings
4	Guitars	Acoustic/Electric Guitars, Banjo, Mandolin, Dulcimer, Ukulele, Hawaiian Guitar
5	Mallets	Vibraphone, Marimba, Xylophone, Steel Drums, Bells, Celesta, Chimes
6	Liturgical	Pipe Organ, Hand Bells, Vocal Ensemble, Choir, Organ Flutes
7	Bright	Saxophones, Trumpet, Mute Trumpet, Synth Leads, Jazz/Gospel Organs
8	Piano	Piano, Electric Piano, Honky Tonk Piano, Harpsichord, Clavi
9	Novelty	Melodic Percussion, Wah Trumpet, Synth, Whistle, Kazoo, Perc. Organ
10	Bellows	Accordion, French Accordion, Mussette, Harmonica, Pump Organ, Bagpipes